D1356983

C016087999

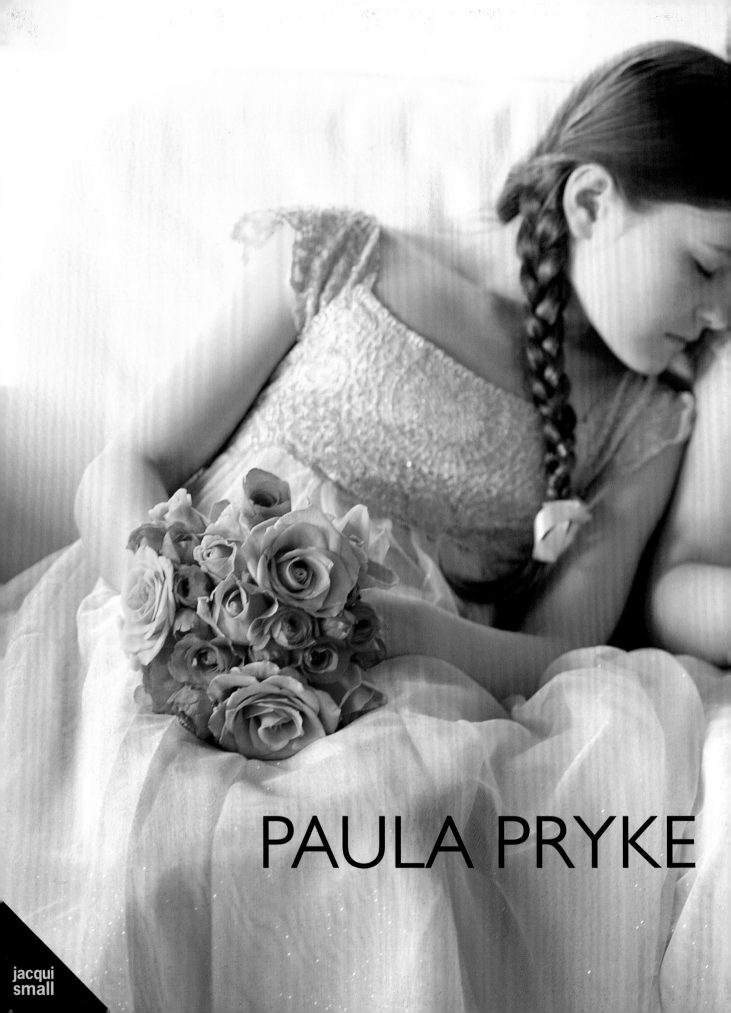

PAULA PRYKE

jacqui
small

WEDDING FLOWERS

Photography by

Tim Winter

*For all my brides and grooms —
past, present and future*

First published in 2014 by
Jacqui Small LLP
an imprint of
Aurum Press Ltd,
74–77 White Lion Street
London N1 9PF

Publisher Jacqui Small
Managing Editor Lydia Halliday
Project Editor Sian Parkhouse
Editorial Assistant Alexandra Labbe Thompson
Designer & Art Director Robin Rout
Photographer Tim Winter
Production Maeve Healy

British Library
Cataloguing-in-Publication Data
A catalogue record for this book
is available from the British Library.

ISBN 978 1 909342 54 5

2016 2015 2014

10 9 8 7 6 5 4 3 2 1

Printed and bound
in China.

Contents

Page 1 A tied trailing bouquet of the gorgeous
scented rose Prince Jardinier with jasmine trails
and camellia.

Pages 2–3 Some sleepy bridesmaids clutch bouquets of bright pink ranunculus with Combo, Bellevue and Carina roses.

This page This fulsome arrangement for the celebrant's table at Fetcham Park, Surrey, includes Black Baccara, Cool Water, Naomi and Peach Avalanche+ roses with lilac, guelder roses, asparagus fern and ruscus. 'Menton' tulips and purple vanda orchids trail over the table.

Left Catherine and New Yorker Ian met in San Francisco. Their London wedding honoured Catherine's English roots, but also proved a fabulous destination for guests from New York and California. The flowers were inspired by the couple's favourite places: roses for England, succulents for California and orchids for South America.

Left Alex and Lucy wanted their flowers to respond to the distinct spaces of the ceremony and reception. In St Bartholomew the Great church in London, blue delphiniums and roses were interwoven around the arched entrance. In the reception venue, Wilton's Music Hall, they combined roses, daisies, sweet peas, moss and sunflowers for a wild and overgrown effect.

Left Sam from Bury St Edmunds, Suffolk, and Jono from New Zealand met in London. They married in Waitakere, New Zealand, and then came back to England for their wedding blessing at Bury St Edmunds Cathedral. Sam chose a blue, white and lilac theme to tie in all the colours of her bridesmaids' dresses.

Introduction

I HAVE BEEN DESIGNING WITH FLOWERS for nearly thirty years. Over that time I have had the pleasure to work on so many gorgeous and diverse weddings with brides and grooms from all over the world. Each one is very special to me and I love the journey of getting to know a couple, and then over a period of time building up a vision of how they want their special celebration to be. The intensity of the relationship often endures beyond the big day, and I have been fortunate to stay in touch and sometimes become life-long friends with my wedding clients.

In my experience, wherever you are, whatever your religious beliefs or values, there is a universal human desire to form a bond and enter into a wedding contract. Although weddings have been declining in numbers, particularly in Europe, I have seen the wedding industry grow enormously in the past decades and it is thriving. I think it is wonderful to witness the union of two people with an intense bond and a desire to approach life as a team. Many of the recent changes in the laws on marriage in different countries have been put forward on the basis of human rights, and the wedding is a glorious celebration of that union and the tastes and styles of the spouses.

I have noticed that when weddings were considered to be quite traditional, and often with a religious element to the ceremony, those who did not want to buy into that generally avoided getting married. Now, with the growth of inter-racial, multi-faith and even same-gender weddings, the diversity of the marriage union is much broader. You can have the wedding you want on your terms and at any budget.

In my years as a florist, I have seen how world travel and transportation and the internet have transformed the wedding business from a local and traditional one to a global phenomenon with a myriad of choices. The multi-million pound industry, with its huge marketing, can be a daunting prospect. The websites, the bloggers, the suppliers and the venues all vie for attention; it is sometimes hard to know just where to start. The global scale is evident to me in every way. Often the bride and groom or partners have met on holiday, or when studying and working abroad. At least one in three weddings that I now have the pleasure of decorating have very different cultural, regional and religious beliefs. Weddings have become a cornucopia of ideas and options and navigating your way to the perfect day has never been harder!

Left Enda and Liz met at work; it was a good old-fashioned case of love at first sight. They chose to get married at Blenheim because, as Liz frankly explained, 'only a palace will do'.

Left Beverley from Bury St Edmunds met Chad from Oxford, Massachusetts, while he was stationed in England at RAF Lakenheath with the US Air Force. They wed in an intimate, candlelit ceremony at the small village church of Dalham where they lived before Chad was posted to South Korea for a year.

Left Matthew from Sydney and Shanyan from Hong Kong were living in London. After a proposal in Paris they decided to tie the knot at Sudeley Castle in the Cotswolds because they both love the English countryside.

What I have noticed is that the global scale of the wedding industry means that the time it takes to plan a wedding has been extended. You may think you are buying a dress from an Italian designer but it may well be made in a factory in China. The chances are that your made-to-measure dress or suit may get shipped from the Far East, and that means some bridal houses like to have six months to prepare your wedding gown. Your flowers may be locally grown, but it is just as likely that they will come from the Netherlands, South America, Kenya or Israel. This mean that you can pretty much have what you want most weeks of the year – if you can afford it! Flower lovers would be astonished to find out how much of their flower costs arise from global transportation. Any rise in oil prices acutely affects the price of flowers, and any major downturn in the market immediately shrinks the supply, as gorgeous flowers are a luxury item.

Being based as a floral designer in London means that I often decorate weddings where the betrothed couples have chosen London as a destination venue for their wedding, and may not actually live in London themselves. Communication is often through email or through a central coordinator or planner. On some rare occasions I have not met the bride and groom until the day of the wedding. I have also been asked to decorate weddings abroad and on boats and ships encircling the world. While the logistics of props and people can be a complication, getting the flowers to a specific place is always easy, thanks to the world flower domination of the Netherlands. As a nation of traders they are pretty excellent at their logistics, too, and I have never been stuck at a destination waiting for my flowers.

Each and every wedding I have had the pleasure to be involved in has a special memory and although I can't always at first remember the people, I always remember the flowers! Weddings are one of the reasons I love my job. What could be better than turning up to a venue with a van load of beautiful flowers and enhancing a wonderful celebration?

For those approaching a wedding, this book tells you all you need to know about how to select your wedding flowers, whether you are doing the flowers yourself or using a floral designer. Thank you to all my previous clients who have let me play a decorative part in the celebration of their unions. Long may weddings endure in all their forms all over the world!

Left Rod Stewart and Penny Lancaster were married in a chapel decorated with white roses in the town of Santa Margherita on the Italian Riviera. 'The flowers complemented the magical day while the theme of feathers used in the flower displays and invitations brought our dream to life,' *Penny.*

Left 'It was simply a gorgeous day; a joyous celebration of love and happiness. And of course, isn't it every girl's dream to be wed in a beautiful castle!' *Shanyan and Matthew*

Left Horseshoes are ancient symbols of good luck. The Greeks were the first to use this symbol as a talisman for newlyweds to enhance fertility. Traditionally. the youngest member of the wedding group presents the shoe to the bride. This horseshoe is covered with pink heather but white is also considered to be very lucky, too.

WEDDING
FLOWERS

Chic Orchids

MINI CYMBIDIUM VARIETIES

VANDA 'SUNANDA CHOCOLATE BROWN'

VANDA 'EXOTIC PURPLE'

VANDA 'CERISE MAGIC'

VANDA 'SUNANDA EXOTIC PURPLE'

PHALAENOPSIS

DENDROBIUM 'WALTER'

PAPHIOPEDILUM

PAPH

ORCHIDS ARE ONE of the most stylish flowers on the planet. These beguiling, enticing flowers grow in nearly every country in the world and every climate from the desert to the Arctic, so there is an immense variety.

With an astounding number of varieties, orchids are available throughout the world all the year round, making them a very popular choice. Once thought of as exotic, these long-lasting and prolific plants have become commonplace in our homes and workplaces. The interesting and intricate flowers are associated with love, luxury, exotic beauty, intimacy and with endurance and strength – all good associations for your wedding celebration. Orchids are elegant and graceful, and with so many to choose from there is bound to be one that works with your colour preference and style.

Previous pages, left Potted lily of the valley line a reception table. **Right** *Paphiopedilum maudiae*, known commonly as a lady's slipper orchid.

The flatter faces of
vanda and phalaenopsis
orchids, such as Balan's
Kaleidoscope, make them
easier to mix with other
flower varieties and also
more suitable to be wired
into long trailing bouquets.

Wired 'Tayanee Blue' and 'Springtime Blue' vanda orchids and purple-tinged succulents form a colourful bridal bouquet edged with galax leaves.

This gargantuan family has an estimated 22,500 species and more than 100,000 hybrids, and obsessional growers produce new hybrids each year. The ancient Greeks associated orchids with virility, but by the time they had become popular in Victorian Britain they were a symbol of luxury. The Aztecs and the Chinese prized them for their healing properties. There is something so seductive, tantalizing and alluring about orchids that I think of them as one of my favourite wedding flowers.

Price depends on the time of year and the variety you fall in love with. At the less expensive end of the scale you could choose the massively overproduced phalaenopsis orchids. A simple two-stemmed plant makes a stunning yet frugal choice for a wedding centrepiece. A planted phalaenopsis can flower for at least six months, and so it makes a perfect gift for your guests after the wedding is over. Or you can start your own orchid collection and have a living keepsake from your wedding. Phalaenopsis orchids in their natural habitat grow under the canopy of trees in tropical climates. The stems hang down from the roots of the plant, and so they have the perfect habit for trailing wedding bouquets – nine stems tied together make a stunning bouquet.

Rare and relatively more expensive would be the cattleya orchids, a genus of 41 species that were originally discovered in the tropical climate of South America. Their flowers make showy corsages and can be the focal flowers in larger arrangements.

The most common cut flower is the cymbidium orchid. Long-stemmed cymbidiums can be striking in large pedestal displays. Mini cymbidiums are a much more delicate flower and also more affordable. They are perfect for buttonholes or wiring into corsages, headdresses and bouquets.

More recently the most fashionable orchid has been the vanda. When I wrote my second book we photographed the first one I had ever seen. A little later I went to the Aalsmeer Flower Show and saw them trialled. They are now widely available. At first it was the violet colour and marking that made them so popular, but now you can buy them in white, cream, pink, lilac, purple, orange, brown and black.

There are 800 species of oncidium orchids, but the most common are the yellow, russet and brown varieties. They have lots of small flowers on long, thin graceful stems that appear to dance in the breeze, hence their common name of 'dancing ladies'. These plants look amazing massed together in big displays and also as single flowers in bud vases.

Highly prized and extremely photogenic is the *Paphiopedilum* slipper orchid. The colour is more subdued than some of its cousins, but it is the distinctive slipper-like lip and its markings that always make me swoon when I open a box! Personally, I adore the green and white varieties, but there are gorgeous mauve and golden varieties too. Their shape is so strong they look best on their own as a buttonhole or in individual vases.

Another large and diverse genus of orchids are the dendrobium orchids. These were originally from diverse habitats in South East Asia, Australia and New Zealand. This group is often referred to by florists as 'Singapore Orchids', as the vast majority of cut flowers are exported from Singapore to flower markets all over the world. Dendrobiums are very useful flowers for wiring into wedding work. I love to thread them onto long wires and use them en masse as a hanging decoration. They work well in bridal bouquets and also look good as a single flower head laid on a napkin.

Slipper orchids are so exotic and distinct in shape that they suit very modern and minimal designs. This cultivar of *Paphiopedilum insigne* perfectly inspires an autumn colour palette.

Not only are orchids beautiful but some also have amazing fragrance. The cattleyas are the most highly prized for scent – some are floral and citrus and some have more of a cinnamon or vanilla fragrance. Most cymbidiums have a sweet and heady perfume and phalaenopsis a faint lemon scent.

The ubiquitous white phalaenopsis orchid has been so over-produced in the Netherlands that sometimes supply exceeds demand. In a desperate bid to sell more cut white phalaenopsis, they have been forced to drink plant dyes. The vibrant colours can be seen coursing through their veins. Interestingly, dyed flowers do cause a stir, particularly when it is the first time that flower is seen in a new colour. If you are planning an evening party with a real dance-club feel that is going to be heavily lit with coloured gels, you might as well go for something eye-catching, such as these dyed phalaenopsis. Most hotel ballrooms are often windowless and there is always a heavy use of spotlights to enhance the flowers. This is an important consideration when choosing floral decorations, as subtle colours are often lost. Brightly coloured flowers, monochromatic schemes and white flowers work the best in these environments.

White phalaenopsis
orchids have been given
dyes to drink, creating
neon colours.

MISTY BUBBLES SPRAY ROSE

DARLEY

TENGA-VENGA

CATALINA SPRAY ROSE

CRÈME DE LA CRÈME

SPUTNIK!

BLUE GENE

WANTED

SUDOKU

CHERRY-O!

PUMPKIN

WILD DOG ROSE

FAIR DIAMOND

Rich Roses

THROUGHOUT HISTORY roses have enhanced and improved our lives. They grace all our important ceremonies and celebrations, and are by far and away the most popular and appealing choice for weddings.

The reasons for this are legion. Firstly, the rose, above all flowers, is a symbol of love and romance. The ancient Greeks and Romans were the first to choose roses to adorn their celebrations, and they thought nothing of strewing roses a foot deep on the ground as if it had been raining roses! Standing on the scented petals would have made the room intoxicating with scent. The ancient Greeks and Romans identified the rose with the goddesses of love, Aphrodite and Venus. My favourite story concerns Emperor Nero, who held the most lavish parties, with roses and the scent of rose oil everywhere. At one party it was recorded that guests suffocated under a deluge of rose petals that had been released into the air. Nero's extravagance with roses was said to be one of the reasons that the Roman Empire collapsed.

Rose lovers you have been warned!

Opposite Viburnum berries with Cool Water, Grand Prix and Black Baccara roses give this hand-tied bouquet an autumnal twist. *Daucus carota* 'Dara' adds a vintage feel.

Opposite A densely packed heart of pink Wham, Pearl Avalanche+ roses and spray roses, yellow Catalina spray roses and Caraluna garden roses, interspersed with the tropical vine *Diplocyclos palmatus*, rosemary leaves and feathery astilbe flowers.

The main reason that roses are so popular is simply because they are such good-looking, reliable flowers, available fifty-two weeks of the year. There are over 100 species and tens of thousands of varieties. Relatively long-lasting, they are a good shape for working into many different designs. Their gorgeous petally shape can work well in both loose and more formal arrangements, and so you can find these wonderful flowers used in many varied wedding schemes. They can look modern and chic for a contemporary interior or traditional for a historic venue.

Another reason roses are so popular is for their fragrance. Not all commercially grown roses have a scent, but some do, and this can be another significant reason for them being the first choice for brides. The rose oil that is distilled from the petals makes a lovely scent used in candles to add to the cloakrooms and corridors of your wedding venue to delight the senses. It is said that Cleopatra wooed Mark Anthony with rose oil and rose petals, and certainly today's lovers know all about the seductive power of a bunch of roses.

Above right A basket lined with buttonholes of Pearl Avalanche+ roses with Fair Diamond rosehips, edged with the grey leaves of *Brachyglottis* 'Sunshine'.

In recent years the demand for pink, lilac, taupe and green roses has produced a number of new varieties, and there has also been a huge trend in growing old-fashioned garden roses on a commercial level. The choice is immense, with the vast majority being cultivated in South America. New varieties appear all the time, giving floral designers a new palette of colours. Often, if a new variety is popular and reliable it will then appear in a number of colours. For example, the white rose Avalanche+ was followed by Sweet Avalanche+, which is pink, and there are now Peach, Pearl, Candy, Emerald, Sorbet and spray versions.

A good modern classic rose for the commercial world needs to have strong stems, a high petal count and a fully opening head. Miss Piggy fits this bill. Named after the character in *The Muppets*, this is a strong rose that lasts a long time in the vase and opens fully. Its colour-shaded petals can be a feature in weddings, used as scented confetti or sprinkled on the table.

Above left Miss Piggy is a diva rose. Large-headed with coral petals that are peach in the centre and pink on the edge, it makes a stunning rose to use in monochromatic schemes as well as working well with bright pink.

Above and right This outdoor table has been dressed with a vase placed inside a glass vase filled with wedding confectionery. A domed posy of Miss Piggy roses sits in the centre vase, which is filled with water. Single roses are tucked under the napkins, and petals and sweets are scattered over the table to complete the theme.

The rose can be used in many different designs and it mixes well with other scented wedding flowers, such as jasmine, gardenia, lily of the valley and stephanotis. It wows when used in monochromatic schemes and also combines well with mixed colours. The different varieties, sizes and scales of the rose make it useful in delicate designs as well as huge grand designs. Some roses can be grown as tall as 2m (6 feet).

Below Late garden roses have been given an autumnal twist with rosehips, ornamental kales, grasses and ivies. Small apples, groups of kumquats and bunches of grapes add colour and texture.

The rose is also incredibly photogenic – most flowers are, but some are born to love the camera more. It is hard to take a bad photo of a rose. For this reason, the dome of roses is often the chosen floral accessory for an advertising or editorial shoot, and this intensifies their supreme position among the wedding flower hierarchy.

Rosehips should not be forgotten, particularly as they are now available in thirty different varieties in the autumn and come in long lengths. They inspire floral designs and are very decorative when used with roses and with other flowers. As a textural plant material they are very current and in vogue.

Opposite This beautiful candelabra arrangement was part of a Valentine's Day wedding at the Grosvenor House in London. Sweet Akito and Anna roses, Pepita spray roses, pale pink clonal ranunculus and white hydrangea are set off by green trailing amaranthus and asparagus fern. Rosemary-covered containers round the base have been filled with hyacinths, white dill and olive foliage.

'KILIMANJARO' GERBERA

'BOURNIER' SANTINI CHRYSANTHEMUM

'WHITE GRIZZLY' GERBERA

SINGLE TANACETUM

LEUCANTHEMUM X SUPERBUM 'BECKY'

'MADIBA' SANTINI CHRYSANTHEMUM

MATRICARIA

Pretty Daisies

AN UNDERSTATED AND INNOCENT FLOWER associated with purity and
simplicity, the classic daisy is a yellow centre or disc with white ray florets or
petals. This pleasing shape is designed by nature to be as attractive as it can
to insects. It is also perennially popular as a wedding flower.

My favourite cut-flower daisies are the ox-eye daisies, or marguerite daisies.
Native to the Canary Islands, *Argyranthemum frutescens* are a more hardy cut
flower and a very useful plant. If you want a more delicate wild-flower look,
you may consider the *Tanecetum* daisies, a genus that includes feverfew.
These have a lovely herby scent and are a useful cut flower in jam jars and
simple containers, but are too fragile to be wired. Another delicate daisy
is the September or Michaelmas daisy. These long stems with lots of small
heads look best en masse. They are also useful for filling jugs and watering
cans as casual decorations, and as a filler for mixed arrangements. When
I first started my flower business my mother grew me *Pyrethrum* daisies
to sell, now classified as *Tanacetum coccineum*. For several months in the
summer you can procure very strong and reliable *Leucanthemum* daisies,
mostly grown in the Netherlands. Some of these are single daisies with
yellow centers such as *Leucanthemum* x *superbum* 'Becky' and *Leucanthemum
vulgare* 'Maikönigin'. Others are doubles such as 'Ester Read' and 'Wirral
Supreme'. All these cultivars are amazingly strong and have a really good
vase life. Daisies mix well with other 'wild' looking flowers such as dill and
quaking grass, but I think also work very well with garden roses.

A sweet bridesmaid's basket of stephanandra, snowberry and white 'Star of Billion' astrantia, with fronds of the yellow dill *Anethum graveolens* and *Leucanthemum* x *superbum* 'Becky' daisies. Dill, being another wild flower, is one of my favourite partners for daisies – it makes the yellow disc of the daisy centre pop with colour.

The other daisies I have considered for this section are gerberas and the chrysanthemum spray daisies. These are both widely available in many colours all year round, making them a very good choice for brides. There are countless horticultural varieties of chrysanthemum, and several that resemble the common daisy shape, with a yellow centre and white petals. There are also many other colours with the same basic shape, including red, brown, green and orange. Chrysanthemums are robust flowers and can be used in wired work as well as in massed design. This makes them very useful if you wanted to inscribe your names together for your wedding, or make round topiary balls or trees.

Below This long, rectangular glass vase has holes all along the top of it, making it perfect for supporting daisy-shaped flowers such as gerberas. 'Lemon Ice', 'Kermit' and the pink 'Kimsey' have been arranged with swirls of the variegated green lily grass, *Liriope muscari* 'Variegata'.

Above right One of the newest chrysanthemum varieties is a very small-headed santini. These have shorter stems and denser flower heads, so they work well in hand-tied bouquets. The smaller daisy varieties also work well massed together, and these ice cream cones have been made with 'Madiba' white chrysanthemums with green centres.

The most useful commercial daisy is the gerbera. They have an irresistible charm and innocence. Vita Sackville-West, the English writer and gardener, first spotted them in a florist shop and discovered that they were called the Transvaal daisy or gerbera. Although the name did not please her, the flower certainly did, and she remarked how they came in any colour one could desire. She died in 1962 when gerberas were just becoming a popular cut flower. Since then they have become one of the top five cut-flower varieties. Gerberas are available in thousands of colours and vary in face width from 7cm (2½ inches) for the Germini varieties to over 12cm (4½ inches) for the standard heads. Robust enough to stand external and internal wiring, they work well in topiaries and large arrangements as well as simple bouquets.

A rustic stand is topped with a topiary wreath frame of ivy to provide a base for a daisy ring with its own bow. A touch of asparagus fern was added to lighten the foliage. The flower heads are all individually placed in small plastic phials of water to keep them alive. The bow was made from chicken wire and ivy trails, decorated with *Leucanthemum* x *superbum* 'Becky' and 'Bournier' Santini chrysanthemums.

Blowsy Dahlias

DAHLIAS HAVE A HUGE FANBASE ALL OVER THE WORLD, mainly because these showy tubers have adapted so well and can be grown in so many countries. They reward the gardener with a profusion of flashy flowers whose repeat flowering is enviable.

Visit any flower show or farmers' market in the northern hemisphere in August and September and you are likely to see the indispensable dahlia in its many guises and colours. Originating in Central America, these intoxicating beauties arrived in Europe at the end of the eighteenth century. The first European tubers were planted in the botanical gardens in Madrid, where they were named after a Swedish botanist called Anders Dahl. Their beautiful flower heads come in an astonishing range of shapes, including peony, waterlily, orchid, anemone and chrysanthemum, not to mention all the different formations of their petals. Some of my favourites are the rounded Pompons and the flashy cactus varieties.

It was the British during the Victorian era, with their huge empire covering a fifth of the world, who exported these tubers into the colonial gardens of the world.

A garden trug filled with elderberries, autumnal apples, *Viburnum opulus* berries and 'New Orange' dahlias, mixed with garden roses and strong pink *Dianthus barbatus* (sweet William).

A bridesmaid's bouquet of deep red
peonies, eupatorium, nigella seed heads,
dusty pink echinacea daisies and pale
pink 'Wizard of Oz' dahlias.

Right This neat hand-tied bridesmaid's posy is of 'Diana's Memory' dahlias. Their delicate pink shading with green-tinged centres really shows up when they are used on their own and they make a great foil for the dark blue of the bridesmaid's dress.

The Victorians helped to make dahlias one of the world's favourite flowers. Now the export of dahlia tubers from the Netherlands to the rest of the world is a significant part of the horticultural export trade. There are some 50 million tubers or roots sent overseas each year to every country that has a climate that can grow them. Seen everywhere from stately homes to tower block balconies, from municipal parks to royal palaces, this is a flower that is both easy to grow and makes a terrific cut flower. There are over 10,000 varieties, and although there are lots of lavender, mauve and purple shades the one colour that still eludes the hybridizers is the colour blue.

One of the reasons dahlias are enjoying a massive renaissance of interest at the moment is that they are one of the few flowers that the supermarket and the multiple retailers can't deal with. They are too petally to survive the rigours of mass packing and transportation, and so they largely remain a garden flower or a bloom that you have to procure through a florist, farmers' market or specialist grower. This makes them a precious jewel, romantic and irresistible.

Dahlias are generally in season from June to December. 'Wizard of Oz' is a pale pink cultivar that does well as a cut flower and is especially suitable for wedding bouquets and table arrangements. Dahlias can be wired into buttonholes, but they do shatter easily and so the first hug may render them pot pourri!

Right One of the darkest dahlias is 'Karma Naomi', and these look sensational when wired onto bridesmaids' accessories. The jewel colours of the bridesmaid's bouquet, which includes 'Carolina Wagermanns', 'Orfeo', 'Witteman's Best', 'Black Wizard' and 'David Howard' dahlias, work well with bold fabric or gown choices.

Perfect Ranunculus

THE PERFECT CHOICE for brides planning a winter or spring wedding, ranunculus are stunning and available in a huge range of colours. These romantic rosette flowers have an enormous petal count and look like an origami masterpiece made from crepe paper.

I probably owe my career as a florist to the sighting of these beauties in a shop window in the Swiss ski resort of St Moritz. I was already contemplating a career change to floristry when in the spring of 1987 I went skiing with my then fiancé, Peter. Beguiled by the window display of these brightly coloured petally flowers, which I had never previously set eyes on, I had an epiphany. I determined to change from being a history teacher to a florist, and eighteen months later I opened my first flower shop. These gorgeous flowers became a focus of devotion that has now spanned three decades. Gazing at the mix of colours in that shop window was a really important lesson in colour design for me. Although they appear to clash, the ranunculus looked so harmonious. That day I learnt that if you use brightly coloured flowers of the same intensity, with the absence of white or pale colours, the effect will arrest and delight.

As they are an expensive flower, ranunculus rarely make it into supermarkets. They are very delicate and their thin petals bruise easily. This means that they are treasured and rare, and so are popular for special events such as weddings. I am grateful for that – their high worth and limited season keep them very special.

ELEGANCE SERIES PASTEL PINK

'GLAMOROUS PINK'

'MISTRAL SALMON'

HANOI

'PAULINE GOLD'

'MISTRAL APRICOT'

'PAULINE VIOLET'

Opposite I still adore the simple multicoloured ranunculus that can be grown in Cornwall for a short season. These often appear just in time for my birthday in late April. A box has been an annual indulgence each year. This vibrant rounded dome contains green Pon Pon Series 'Flora', 'Pauline Dark Orange', Elegance Series ranunculus in violet, yellow and pink.

An elegant boat-shaped table arrangement of
'Glamorous Pink' and Elegance Series pastel pink
ranunculus in varying stages of opening among
Viburunum tinus blossom and ivy trails.

A short-stemmed flower, barely over 50cm (20 inches), ranunculus are the perfect wedding bloom for posies, buttonholes and table centres. The season in Europe starts around November and goes on to June. They are part of the huge *Ranunculaceae* family and are direct relations to the common buttercup, *Ranunculus acris*.

Cut-flower ranunculus are grown mainly in Italy, where they have been improving their production each year. They are also widely grown in the Netherlands, Israel and California. Small local growers are dotted around the world, but after the Italians, it is the Japanese who have been wowing the New York flower market with some of the best ranunculus.

Standard ranunculus come in many colours. The Italians call the speckled varieties cappuccino, and they come in yellow and pink. The Californians call the pink-and-white frosted ranunculus Merlot and Flamenco is the name for the picotee variety, which is yellow flecked with red. These feminine flowers with layers of petals last around eight to ten days. It is the white or the soft pastel ranunculus that are of the most interest to the bridal industry. 'Hanoi', a gorgeous pale pink variety in the Success range, is perfect for wedding bouquets. These pale ranunculus, almost the size of peonies, look stunning when mixed with lily of the valley or soft spring foliage such as guelder rose or lilac blossom. For the daring bride there is always the deep burgundy ranunculus. I once did a wonderful jewel-coloured wedding with burgundy 'Pauline Violet' mixed with bright pink roses, purple and burgundy 'Bordeaux' anemones and textural succulents. The more expensive ranunculus are called clonal, often called *cloni* (Italian for clones), Clooney or Clone-y. Standard Extra quality and Ranunculus Success Series have been making their way into the flower markets of the world and the costs are as spectacular as the flowers. Venere is a stunning double in apricot and cream and 'Sangria' is orange coloured with a stunning green eye. The new Pon-Pon Series are ruffled, with huge heads, and also come in speckled varieties. 'Hermione' is a pink, white and green striped variety.

The Californian ranunculus growers have a very long season – the dry climate is perfect for these tuber-grown flowers. Any ranunculus fan should make the pilgrimage to Carlsbad, south of San Diego, to see the rainbow fields in March and April. Ranunculus the size of peonies are grown in vast fields in single colours and mixed colours to make a stunning visual feast. The Tecolote tubers produce several flowers, with heads as wide as 10cm (5 inches). Many California doubles are the result of the breeding efforts of Edwin Frazee of The Flower Fields in Carlsbad, and this is certainly a vision of heaven on earth for me!

Below 'Glamorous Pink' and 'Elegance Pastel Pink' ranunculus are the perfect colour to set off the brown of Cosmos's coat, as she serves patiently as an attendant. Pets are increasingly popular guests at weddings.

Above The papery petals of Hanoi combine with the unusual multicolours of Ranunculus Success Felicidade and Ranunculus Success Lemon.

Opposite Ranunculus Success Series Pauline Gold and Flamenco set in green cubes and around rustic candelabras.

Timeless Tulips

TULIPS ARE WIDELY LOVED all over the world and are a daily purchase in our flower selection throughout their season, which is from November to June.

Although tulips were originally grown in the royal gardens of the Ottoman Empire, they derive their name from a Persian word that means turban-covered head. This is a picturesque description of their distinctive shape. The flowers were much admired in Europe, where they became an instant success in the middle of the seventeenth century, culminating in 'tulipmania'. At this time bulbs changed hands for preposterous sums of money. One attraction was the fact that viruses would cause plain varities to break from an earlier form and the new plant would have unique new markings and colours. We now know that this was in fact a viral infection, but at the time it sent the collectors into a frenzy of speculation. For several years the market boomed and inflated, but inevitably a crash came in 1637 and many lives were ruined by bankruptcy.

DOUBLE V

'SUPERGREEN' PARROT TULIP

DOUBLE PINK 'DALADIER'

'MENTON' TULIP

'FLAMING PARROT'

There are an enormous variety of tulips available and they are generally classified by the period when they bloom, such as early- or late-flowering tulips. You can get standard tulips, double tulips, ballet tulips with pointed petals, peony flowering, serrated-edged and Parrot tulips. The last three have very ruffled petals, and parrot tulips usually have the most amazing markings. Most of these tulips are around or under 50cm (20 inches) in height, which makes them ideal for bouquets and table centres. Tulips are not easy to wire, as the petals often shatter, and they are too fragile to make them useful as a buttonhole.

Left A simple round bouquet of 'Menton' tulips makes an elegant springtime wedding bouquet.

Opposite The ring around the base of this candelabra includes the double red tulip 'Red Princess' on a bed of black viburnum berries and ivy berries. Black Baccara roses and red *Scabiosa atropurpurea* from Israel give texture and depth to the design. The scabious heads have also been laid on the napkins.

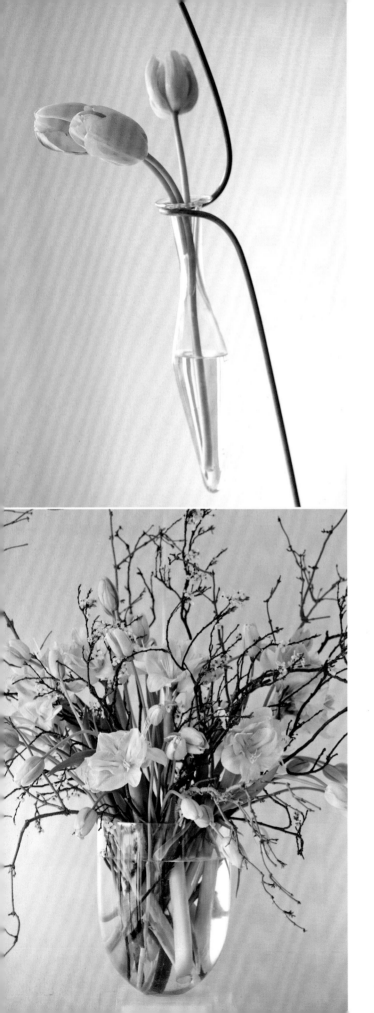

The most stylish and elegant tulips are the French or the Californian tulips, which are 60 to 85cm (23 to 33 inches) in length. These long-stemmed tulips can be lovely in a casual over-arm bouquet. My favourites at present are 'Menton', which is peach, 'Menton Extra' and the pale yellow 'Maureen'. The short tulips mix well with other spring flowers such as ranunculus, lilac, guelder roses, hyacinths and anemones. My personal favourite are the fringe-edged varieties and you can see a bridal bouquet with 'Honeymoon' tulips on page 115. I also adore 'Cuban Night', which is serrated and the colour of aubergine.

Tulips of all types are available in a kaleidoscope of colours, including striped and two-tone varieties. I like the pale pink single 'Candy Pink' and the double 'Angélique'. Favourites include the orange 'Prinses Irene', yellow 'Monte Carlo' and the yellow-and-red striped 'Monsella'. Multicoloured red 'Rococo' and white-and-green 'Super Green' have been favourite parrot varieties for a while, but my current top Parrot is 'Libretto'. A mixture of peach, pink and cream with a touch of green, it reminds me of a selection of *gelato* in Italy!

Tulips are a very meritocratic flower. They look as good in a jug on your kitchen table as they do in a Dutch Old Master painting. I love to use them en masse, rather than in a mixed arrangements, as they continue to grow when cut and will grow taller than the other flowers. Their natural inclination to continue growing in water makes them challenging even when arranged on their own, but I like the interaction with the natural flow of nature. If you are planning a DIY wedding and you want to use tulips, it is best to use them on their own. If you do want to use them in a mixed bunch cut them a little shorter than the rest of the flowers, and keep them as cool and out of the light as you can before displaying them. This way the tulips won't take off higher than the rest of the flowers into the light and sun!

Above left Elegant heads of 'Menton' tulips make the perfect flower for these narrow bottles that line the aisle.

Left and opposite This stylish spring ceremony was inspired by Swedish fabric designer Bitte Stenström, who designed the fabric on the bride's and groom's chairs. Bitte was out walking on the island of Öland admiring the bare branches of the trees and dreaming of springtime. I used mossy twigs from leafless trees as well as some early-flowering prunus for this wedding, with 'Rilona' amaryllis in the central urn – the perfect colour to combine with the tulips. Two huge glass columns placed either side of the urn were filed with 2-m (6-feet) high branches of pussy willow and swirls of extra tall 'Menton' tulips.

Elegant Lilies

'LUCILLE'

THERE ARE SO MANY wonderful varieties of lilies to choose from, from the showy orientals to the slim and elegant callas. There is one to suit every bridal scheme and theme.

Lilies are refined and sophisticated flowers that have been popular throughout history, and they are still a favourite flower for celebrations and events. The oriental lilies suit grand arrangements and have a gorgeous heady scent. *Lilium longiflorum*, which is trumpet shaped, has long been an emblem of purity – it has associations with the Virgin Mary and is thought to be quite sacred in ecclesiastical circles. This makes it a special flower for church weddings of any denomination. The Madonna lily is also associated with Easter and if you are getting married in a church on Easter Sunday it is very likely that lilies will be part of the festival decorations.

Opposite I love to use lilies in pedestal arrangements and other large-scale designs. This one is the Oriental lily 'Mero Star'. But sometimes people do not like the scent or find that the pollen makes them sneeze. Hay fever sufferers often request to have them left off the wedding flower list for that reason.

'SIBERIA'

'ALFIERI'

44

The gorgeous soft pink and lemon 'Papiljo' lily has been arranged with Sudoku roses, *Molucella laevis*, *Viburnum opulus* blossom, arching stephanandra, variegated trails of ivy and green trailing amaranthus. This combination is a wedding classic. Lilies are available all year round but they peak in the summer when there are more varieties available and they are often stronger. The pollen does stain clothes, so removing the stamens is essential in wedding arrangements, in case guests brush past them.

It was the Romans who originally brought this lily to England, believing its sap was therapeutic to soldiers who suffered pain after long marches. Oriental and *longiflorum* lilies last well, and you may have to procure them as many as ten days before a wedding if you want them to be in peak condition. The smaller-headed star-shaped lilies are known as Asiatic and they are not so interesting for weddings – they don't have such a good scent and they are not as showy. However, they are less expensive, so you may want to consider them if your budget is limited.

Lilies are graded according to length and the number of heads. The tallest lilies are over a metre (3 feet), and these are the ones I adore to use in big pedestals and church arches. They are dramatic and a star shape is often a good addition to a flower combination. When I got married in 1987 one of the newest lilies was the now famous 'Star Gazer' and the scent of that lily transports me back to the day. It was a new introduction at the time as Orientals up to that point had downward flowers, and so had a tendency to snap when transported or used. Still available, this star-shaped lily is speckled deep pink with a white edge and was the leader of the pack of many new varieties. There are over a hundred species and countless crosses, as lilies are easy to breed because they are anatomically simple. Until recently, most lilies had three petals and three sepals, making them look like a six-pointed star, but the newest varieties are the doubles, which are multi-petalled.

Callas

COMMONLY KNOWN as calla or arum lilies, these zantedeschia lilies are striking and cool. They are in demand all over the world for weddings, and flower designers like to work with the supermodel of the flower world. Elegant and tall, these flowers lend themselves very well to weddings and bridal work. I adore using the pure white varieties, but they are now available in a wide range of colours, from pale lemon through to egg yellow, pale pink through to beetroot and black, blush to mango. There are gorgeous green callas such as 'Green Goddess' and the speckled green and white 'Tinkerbell'. You can procure callas most of the year, although the supply can be limited or patchy at the start of the year and sometimes towards the end. I have had brides who are desperate to use callas, and sometimes it has been difficult to find some or we have paid a lot more than when the supply is plentiful. Unusual colours and longer-stemmed callas are the most prized and also the most expensive.

Above *Zantedeschia* 'Purple Haze' hand tied into a round bouquet.

ZANTEDESCHIA AETHIOPICA 'WHITE DREAM'

ZANTEDESCHIA 'SHIRAZ'

ZANTEDESCHIA 'PURPLE HAZE'

ZANTEDESCHIA 'CAPTAIN ROMANCE'

This hand-tied bridal bouqet uses 'Crystal Blush' white callas.

Grand Peonies

'MONSIEUR JULES ELIE'

'RED CHARM'

'SARAH BERNHARDT'

'BRIDAL SHOWER'

'PETER BRAND'

'PINK GIANT'

'SARAH BERNHARDT'

'DUCHESSE DE NEMOURS'

'SARAH BERNHARDT'

'RED CHARM'

'RED CHARM'

'SHIRLEY TEMPLE'

PEONIES ARE ONE OF THOSE CLASSIC FLOWERS that are perfectly suited to any celebration, but they are immensely popular for weddings. They are spectacular flowers with a sweet fragrance, and they look at home whether arranged simply in a jug on a table or in an ornate urn in a palace.

Peonies are grand but simple. These gorgeous flowers have beguiled generations since time began, and they still have a mystique about them that elevates them above ordinary flowers and makes them ethereal. They are as venerated as cherry blossom – in China and Japan, enthusiasts flock to peony festivals in their thousands.

Early travellers to China claimed they had seen a gigantic flower shaped like a flowering rose but without any of the thorns. Now the height of fashion, peonies are available in an astonishing 3,000 varieties as a garden plant, but only 200 varieties are grown commercially as a cut flower. Although you can use tree peonies as cut flowers their longevity is short once cut and it is the herbaceous peonies that have long been cultivated as cut flowers. However, the ease of cultivation in a wide range of climates has meant that their season as a cut flower has been considerably lengthened. I have flown peonies in from New Zealand for a London wedding in November, when none could be procured from the local flower markets. My bride was over the moon! They did pretty well following their twenty-four-hour flight halfway across the world, but it is never quite the same as having a locally grown bloom in its prime season. Remember that flowers out of season or airfreighted long distances are rather like asparagus or strawberries out of season – never quite as delightful as you remember them.

Opposite A bridesmaid's bouquet of 'Duchesse de Nemours' peonies edged with variegated hosta leaves.

Opposite A collection of herbacous peonies, including deep red-pink 'Karl Rosenfield', bright pink 'Kansas', 'Coral Sunset', 'Coral Charm', the pale pink 'Chiffon Parfait' and 'Red Charm'.

Peonies mainly come in shades including deep red, deep and pale pink, soft yellows, cream, white and peach. My favourite red peonies are 'Red Charm'. For loud pinks, I pick 'Karl Rosenfield' and 'Kansas'. Mid pinks I often specify for weddings are 'Dr Alexander Flemming', 'Monsieur Jules Elie', 'James Kelway' and, by far the most productive as a cut flower, 'Sarah Bernhardt'. 'Duchesse de Nemours' is a divine white peony.

The sought-after coral peony, *P. mascula* subsp. *mascula*, is such an exquisite shade that I have to use it as much as I can when it is available. There is nothing quite its equal – it is truly irresistible to me. It is semi-double, whereas most of the cut-flower peonies tend to be double varieties, and it has a yellow centre that makes me want to experiment with buttermilk yellow combinations.

Getting the peony at exactly the right condition on the day can be tricky. Really you need to buy peonies five days before you want to use them, but sometimes, depending on when and where they are cut and how long they have travelled, they can take much longer to open. The terrifying thing about letting them open ahead of time is that when they die they shatter and disappear.

Above 'Red Charm' peonies are used in a mixed topiary arrangement with 'Wizard of Oz' dahlias, eupatorium, nigella seed heads and bubble-gum-coloured gerberas with a black eye.

Left A 'Shirley Temple' bud before it bursts into full bloom.

Fragrant Favourites

Lily of the valley

The scented flower of choice for the royalty of Europe and many sophisticated weddings across the globe, lily of the valley is usually in season in late April and May, though it is available all the year round grown under glass. It is a delicate and small flower, so you need a lot of it to make a bouquet or an arrangement look impressive. Long lily of the valley is sold by the stem and is usually shipped on the root, or sometimes in pots or trays, so that it is only cut at the last moment. The stem price does not vary enormously, but it does get slightly less expensive in its season and at that time you can usually get cheaper bunches of much shorter stems. Even in season it will be an expensive option, but you will be joining a long list of royal European princesses who have chosen this flower to be included in their wedding bouquets.

Opposite Lily of the valley has become perhaps one of the most iconic wedding flowers because of the celebrity of the brides that have chosen to include it in their bouquets, including the Duchess of Cambridge, Grace Kelly, Carolyn Bessette when she married John F Kennedy Jr and Lauren Bush when she married David Lauren at Ralph Lauren's ranch.

Left You can buy pots of lily of the valley from February to April, and this is a less expensive way of incorporating it into your wedding.

Stephanotis

Opposite Individually wired fragrant stephanotis pips are edged with a ruffle of sweet peas – add a ring of jasmine and you are in a scented paradise as you walk down the aisle.

This vine produces white waxy star-shaped tubular florets. Originally from Madagascar, it is also known commonly as wax flower, Hawaiian wedding flower or, appropriately, bridal wreath. It has a heady scent and is perfect for wiring into bouquets or for buttonholes. The shiny leaves are also interesting to use in wedding decorations. Other than for its aromatic scent it is often chosen by brides as it is a brilliant white that is rare in flowers, and so it is one to choose if you have a truly white dress. According to the Victorian language of flowers this flower symbolized 'marital happiness', and it is a great choice to include for some fragrance. The plants can also be used to line an aisle or to trail from large arrangements. The pips work well when pinned into hair.

Above Pure and simple: a mass of white freesias and white lilac in a divine white-washed bridesmaid's trug.

Freesias

Freesias have a clean and citrus scent that is very popular. The bell-shaped blooms curve on the stem, making them the perfect shape for a bridal bouquet, and they also look good wired into headdresses and corsages. Originally native to South Africa, they are widely grown commercially as a cut flower in the Netherlands and can be purchased in a huge array of colours. The double-flowered freesia is currently the most popular as it looks much fuller and the petals are more ruffled. They are often more expensive than you might imagine – they retain their exclusivity because the propagation of the corms is a slow business. The snow-white double 'Duet' is one of my favourite of the fifty different double freesias available. March to May is the best time for freesias, but supply is year round.

Sweet peas

With their romantic image sweet peas are the perfect flower to add both scent and colour to your wedding. They are available from around February to September, and peak around June. The most highly scented are the old-fashioned or heirloom varieties. Popular all over the world, they hail originally from Sicily. They are often seen as a quintessential English garden flower, as the British are certainly obsessed and fanatical about growing these delicate flowers with ruffled blossoms. The sugary scent of sweet pea is almost like candy – it is light and fresh and never too heady or overpowering.

Right Sweet peas are too delicate to be wired, and I think they make stunning bridal bouquets used en masse in one colour or in mixed colours. Individual colours also mix well with other flowers for bridal bouquets.

Hyacinths

The heady scent of these flowering bulbs provides a natural room fragrance. Some people feel that they are too heavily scented for a table centre as the smell is a distraction when eating, but they are great to use in the ceremony and also in hallways and entrances to evoke an atmosphere. With densely packed bell-shaped florets, they come in an ever-increasing range of colours. There are great pastel colours and, of course, white and cream and new dynamic bold colours such as the bright pink 'Jan Bos' and the beetroot purple 'Woodstock'. The individual florets can be wired and used to great effect in headdresses and also around napkins.

Left An entrance bowl of pink 'Fondant', blue 'Atlantic' and beetroot 'Woodstock' hyacinths welcome guests with their delicious heady aroma.

This pink and brown arrangement sits on a lacquered silver bowl and includes 'Fondant' hyacinths, 'Bridal Kimsey' Germini gerberas, Sorbet Spray and Sweet Avalanche+ roses and *Prunus*. The brown flocked twigs are mitsumata (*Edgeworthia chrysantha*) from Japan. They are sold bare or stripped, sometimes with coloured flock to add texture to a flower design. The beautiful coordinated menu cards were created by Cutture in London.

Herbs

When you think of scented herbs you often think of mid-summer and all the gorgeous annual herbs that can be cut and used in flower designs. My favourites are the umbelliferous fragrant dill, *Anethum graveolens*, which resembles a lime-green cow parsley. *Daucus carota* 'Dara' is a burgundy-coloured umbellifer that comes from the carrot family. Mint is so refreshing and such a perfect scent for a warm summer's day, and the wild marjoram *Origanum vulgare*, particularly 'Purple Beauty', is another favourite. However, in winter you can still use the evergreen herbs such as bay, rosemary, sage, thyme, juniper and myrtle. Rosemary is one of my favourites for covering containers and using in buttonholes and wedding bouquets. It is a symbol of fidelity as well as remembrance and so it is a popular choice for all kinds of flower designs. Lavender and rosemary can be lovely strewn down the aisle, as when people walk on them they release a fresh fragrance. Myrtle is another very romantic herb with a long history in myth and folklore. Since Queen Victoria carried a sprig in her wedding bouquet, it has been traditionally used in all the weddings of the British royal family. Myrtle is also a favourite plant to be included in the Ukrainian wedding crown.

Above A tumbler, covered with rosemary, is filled with 'Fondant' hyacinths, Sweet Akito roses, Pepita spray roses, *Ammi majus* and *Brachyglottis* 'Sunshine'.

Narcissus

Even though these flowers are seasonal they are among the top five best-selling flowers worldwide, and in the UK they are the number one. I have included them here because they are one of the best scents to use in winter. The production of scented narcissus starts before Christmas, usually in November, and goes on right to the end of March. The white paperwhite (*N. papyraceus*), the pale cream 'Avalanche' and the cream double multi-flowered 'Erlicheer' are some of the first to appear on the market. Each variety has a slightly different fragrance, with 'Avalanche' being more citrus and the 'Erlicheer' being sweeter, more like vanilla custard. Paperwhites work well in bouquets, and the entire narcissus collection looks good en masse or mixed with other early spring flowers. They could be wired into buttonholes – it is important to make sure that the stems are dry before you do this.

Right A trailing garland of ruscus with yellow 'Soleil d'Or' and white paperwhite narcissus and deep blue 'Atlantic' hyacinths creates a scented candelabra.

Lavender

Lavender produces a very clean and fresh scent, which is one of the reasons that the oil is used to scent cleaning products, as well as in aromatherapy for its soothing and relaxing qualities. We often make wedding containers using fresh lavender in May and June when it is plentiful, and dried lavender at other times of the year. I also like to use bunches of lavender tied with raffia or sea grass in decorations. It is an excellent addition to buttonholes and has a very long flowering season, so we have used it as late as October for a wedding. Lavender favours are particularly popular with brides who want to make their own gifts. Originally from the Mediterranean and now extensively grown in Provence and pockets of the English countryside, this scent best suits outdoor or country weddings.

Above *Scabiosa caucasica* 'Lisa' is studded with 'Hidcote' lavender and edged with the felted grey leaves of dusty miller, or *Senecio cineraria*.

Tuberose

Polianthews tuberosa is a night-blooming flower from the agave family, with an exotic scent. It has a long history in the world of perfumery and has been grown in Iran and the South of France for centuries. Tuberose grows about 90cm (35 inches) tall and comes in a pinkish cream colour, with sword-shaped petals on a long straight stem. The flowers are waxy and can be double or single. It often smells better than it looks, and like a lot of scented flowers it is erratic in its vase life. Florets on the stem will start to fade from the bottom up and so it often needs to be picked over to tidy up the stems. Believed to have originated in Mexico, it can be found in many parts of the world. It is not produced in any great quantity, but because it is harvested in many different countries in the southern hemisphere it can be purchased throughout the year.

Left The heavily scented *Polianthes tuberosa* 'Pink Sapphire' decorates a simply tied napkin.

63

WEDDING
THEMES

Above A natural vegetative-style ring of summery foliage and cottage-garden flowers surrounds a white wire candelabra.

Opposite Organic pottery vases display daisies, dahlias and sweet peas. The mixed vases include molucella, dock, *Alchemilla mollis*, zinnias and Avalanche+ spray roses. They also include the seed heads from the dock weeds.

The Right White

WHITE AND GREEN is still the most popular colour choice for weddings and it works very well in both formal and informal settings. For this garden wedding the emphasis was on informal but abundant-looking flowers. The setting for the reception was a large garden with formal borders, but also vast swathes of wild garden.

It also has a very generous productive cutting garden, so I designed the wedding flowers using some organic containers and kept the arranging style very natural and vegetative in some cases. A vegetative flower arrangement places the flowers in the same way that they appear in nature, as if they are growing. However, my clients did not want the flowers to be too informal, so we added a few more formal touches. As this was a mid-summer wedding we had a plentiful selection of wonderful white and green flowers to choose from and daisies, garden roses, sweet peas, white and green alliums and grasses were foremost on our flower list.

Previous pages, left Showering the bride and groom in fresh rose confetti.
Right The city of Bath has a long association with the oak tree and acorns, and so this became one of the themes for a wedding held in the city.

Previous pages The English church that was used for the ceremony dates back to the thirteenth century and has a fine rood screen that was carved in the fifteenth century. Its architectural plan is cruciform, which means that it is in the shape of the cross. This screen made a perfect place to design an indoor arch of white and green flowers and the vicar entrusted me to decorate this unique antiquity. It is essential to always get permission when decorating an historic building. This made the perfect floral frame for the bride and groom when being blessed after their vows.

This wedding used some formal touches, like these massed flowers on the church door and the classic round pomander. It also included some formal pedestals created with long white and green flowers and a wired teardrop-shaped wedding bouquet. Tall candelabras also added a touch of the formal, rather than having all low table displays.

White and green have been popular for wedding flowers since Victorian times and I always think of this combination as very classical. There are some wonderful white flowers to choose from for your wedding bouquet and I used one of my own personal favourites for this wedding. The exquisite Eucharist lily, *Eucharis amazonica*, is from the amaryllis family. It is the purest white with a gorgeous green centre. Its head is a little bowed and it resembles a white daffodil with six pure white petals around a lime-green corona. (You can see this beauty on page 73.) *Eucharis* is from the Greek word for 'grace' or 'charm' and in Latin it means 'elegant', and that really sums up the value of this flower to any wedding scheme. It is not a flower that you see very often in a flower shop, as floral designers for weddings mainly use it, and as it is a tropical plant originally native to Central America and Ecuador. Peonies are another charming white flower and I honestly can't imagine not incorporating them in a summer wedding. On this occasion we used the scented 'Duchesse de Nemours' and 'Shirley Temple'. Scented white sweet peas would also be another must for me.

Left As daisies were a feature flower at this wedding it seemed like a perfect opportunity to make a pomander. These round balls held by small bridesmaids suit round flowers and *Leucanthemum* x *superbum* 'Becky' works perfectly.

Opposite White 'Onesta' dahlias, white 'Duchesse de Nemours' peonies, *Viburnum opulus* and *Leucanthemum* daisies make this massed welcoming wreath on the church door look fluffy and sublime.

Wired natural teardrop bouquet

There is nothing as sophisticated as a wired bridal bouquet. These have fallen from fashion in the last few decades, because the wedding media has pushed natural hand-tied bouquets as they are less expensive and easier to produce for PR work. Wiring a bouquet is a skilled activity and requires patience, labour and time, and you cannot wire the flowers very much in advance of the wedding. It is expensive to produce as every flower has to be removed from its natural stem and placed on a wire. You deconstruct all the flowers and then wire everything back into a constructed bouquet. It is a good idea to practise your wiring technique on smaller projects first, such as buttonholes (see pages 192–93).

INGREDIENTS

7 stems of ivy trails

10 stems of *Panicum* 'Fountain'

5 'Shirley Temple' peonies

10 Eucharist lilies

10 mini phalaenopsis 'Venice'

10 *Eustoma* 'Croma White'

10 stems of *Alchemilla mollis* 'Robusta'

10 stems of hard ruscus

5 stems of *Eucalyptus pulverulenta* 'Baby Blue'

a bunch of galax leaves

a selection of 0.32mm (28 gauge) and 0.28mm (29 gauge) silver wires

some longer 0.71mm (21 gauge) and 0.56mm (23 gauge) wires

a reel of white or green gutta percha tape

a reel of 0.20mm (32 gauge) silver reel wire

2m (78 inches) of white ribbon

1 Sit down with your chosen flowers and foliage and your selection of wires and individually wire each piece of plant material. (See pages 192–93 for how to do this.) Use tissue on your workbench to protect the flowers from bruising and place them in a sturdy pot when they are wired. When everything is wired and taped you are ready to assemble the design. This would usually take around an hour for a bouquet of this size, depending how skilled and fast you are.

2 Establish the tip of the bouquet using some ivy and some *Panicum* 'Fountain'. Begin to introduce the flowers, adding foliage as you go so that you are getting a soft point and a rounded profile. Use a mirror so you can see how it is building up. Keep adding flowers and foliage to build up the height of the bouquet and also the diamond-shaped outline. Think of zig-zagging each variety of flower from the tip to the top at different heights across the display. Keep building up the bouquet until it is about 22–26cm (8½–10 inches) wide. Try to keep all the flowers well balanced throughout the design. Take time to observe the bouquet in the mirror as you build up the flowers and foliage. Bind the bouquet to keep the stems together.

3 When you have completed the bouquet you are ready to add some flowers and foliage to make your 'return end'. This is the floristry term used to describe the flowers that are placed in after the bouquet is completed. This material is placed so it faces back to the top of the bouquet and is more visible for the bride. Leaves then form a ruff, as we have done here with galax, which trail back. Bind all the wires with reel wire at the binding point then bend back the wires to the direction of the tail of the bouquet. Trim the ends of the wires so the handle sits comfortably in the hand and cover with gutta percha tape, then with ribbon. (See page 164, steps 4 and 5.)

This mid-summer bouquet includes seasonal 'Shirley Temple' white peonies with *Alchemilla mollis* 'Robusta' and *Panicum* 'Fountain'.

Above and opposite In mid-summer there are lots of wonderful flowers on the market that are over 1m (3 feet) high. Here we had white eremurus at 1.5m (5 feet) and 1.2-m (4-foot) white delphinium – perfect for large designs like this one.

Grand white pedestal

These wonderful pedestals use lots of foliage to make them look very natural. I adore the contrast of the copper beech foliage with the lime-green molucella and if I can sneak some scented philadelphus into an arrangement I am in heaven as this is one of my favourite summer scents. Don't forget to include some arched or trailing flowers, such as the amaranthus, to give movement.

INGREDIENTS

15 stems of long copper beech (*Fagus sylvatica*) foliage

15 stems of *Molucella laevis*

15 stems of trailing green amaranthus

15 *Philadelphus* 'Snowwhite Fantasy'

15 *Eremurus* 'Foxtrot'

20 *Allium stipitatum* 'White Giant'

20 *Delphinium elatum* 'Snow Queen Arrow'

10 white lilac 'Madame Florent Stepman'

10 *Euphorbia fulgens* 'Quicksilver'

10 *Hydrangea macrophylla* 'Schneeball'

10 'Helvetia' oriental lilies

large urn

large plastic bucket

moss

1 Line the urn with a bucket and moss, then add water with flower food. Begin by establishing the outline of the arrangement with the copper beech. Next use the long spires of molucella to add height and texture.

2 As well as tall and bushy foliage, you also want some with a downward-trailing habit, such as the green amaranthus, and also some arching foliage, such as the philadelphus, to soften the edge of the arrangement. Eremurus adds to the height and good arrangements need lots of variation in shapes.

3 Continue adding the rest of the flowers. The alliums are big globes and also add texture. Keep moving around the arrangement so it will look good from all angles and make sure all the stems radiate from the centre.

4 To finish, lilies are great for filling the gaps. These star-shaped flowers really create impact and add a glorious scent.

1

2

3

4

This beautiful arrangement of white summer flowers has been placed in a birch wreath ring to which we added eucalyptus, viburnums, senecio, now known as *Brachyglottis* 'Sunshine', and a mix of *Echeveria* succulents species. The flowers include zinnias, scabious, tanacetum, love-in-a-mist and *Leucanthemum* x *superbum* 'Wirral Supreme' and 'Becky' and *Leucanthemum vulgare* 'Maikönigin'.

Daisy candelabra

I love the way these simple flowers have been made to look both natural but grand when arranged in a vegetative or growing style around this wire candelabra

INGREDIENTS

a selection of summery foliages: *Panicum*, *Viburnum opulus*, herbs, hebe, *Alchemilla mollis*

20 *Zinnia* 'Lilliput White'

10 *Tanacetum parthenium*

20 *Nigella damascena* double white love-in-a-mist

20 *Nigella damascena* 'Green Magic' love-in-a-mist

20 white *Scabiosa caucasica* 'Anika'

20 *Leucanthemum* x *superbum* 'Wirral Supreme'

20 *Leucanthemum* x *superbum* 'Becky'

45-cm (18-inch) floral foam ring

1 Soak the ring in water with flower food. Taking one of the woody foliages first work your way around the floral foam ring. You need to make sure that some of the foliage is parallel to the table so that the ring is hidden when placed on the table.

2 Build up the foliage using many different types to give it a really natural and wild feel. When working on a design like this you need to take a very holistic approach and be inspired by nature.

3 Start to add some of the softer foliages such as the *Alchemilla mollis* and begin to make the foliages taller, as if growing in the garden. Keep moving around the ring or turning it to view it from all angles.

4 Add the flowers, placing some in at right angles and parallel to the table and then working long stems upwards, as if they are growing towards the light.

5 Add the longer stems of scabious and daisies and, in the words of the famous British floral decorator Constance Spry, leave room for the butterflies!

Opposite Nature is the most wonderful teacher! I imagine walking through a field of ox-eye daisies or along a roadside verge of cow parsley when I take up my scissors to create this type of arrangement.

Handmade Vintage

THERE HAS ALWAYS BEEN an element of vintage or tradition at weddings. In less extravagant times this was often through necessity or custom.

A trousseau or dowry may have consisted of a wedding outfit and also a sort of glory box of treasures for the newly married wife to contribute to her married life. Later this became known as a bottom drawer of inherited or passed on heirlooms. I think the recent trend for vintage hopes to recapture some of the less commercial aspects of the wedding business. It also gives creative or talented brides and grooms the chance to personalize their wedding in a unique way.

This pretty wedding in Bath was the vision of a fine art graduate and her fiancé, a Cambridge veterinary graduate, who met through mutual friends in Cambridge. Their wedding was full of lovely details that were handmade, mostly by the bride, and planning was the key. They asked all their special friends to help them with the decorations and some key tasks at the celebration. The bride and groom both love nature and wanted the flowers to have an English cottage-garden feel. Acorns, oak trees, honeysuckle, herbs and cow parsley came up in our initial discussions and as time went on more and more flowers appeared on their wish list.

Vintage port bottles sourced from antique fairs were filled with Special Reserve port. The table was decorated with ivies, small green apples and the long tendrils of *Gloriosa superba* 'Sparkling Stripe'.

The bride and groom shared the same faith and chose to marry in the bride's family church of Our Lady and St Alphege in Bath. As this special church has some grounds and a garden, they were able to secure permission to place a marquee in the garden and also hire the church hall, providing enough space to accommodate all their friends and family. It was a September wedding and so we were able to use some late summer flowers, including peonies, roses, astilbe, sweet peas and dusty miller. For the church we decided to use some seasonal heritage dahlias and also some vintage chrysanthemum blooms.

Long tables make a cosy style for chatting at the wedding reception and Clare had decided exactly how she wanted her wedding breakfast to look. One of the downsides to long tables is that they are usually quite narrow, and once you have the glassware and cutlery there is not a huge amount of room for floral decorations. Clare sewed table liners and bunting using some hessian fabric and also some lovely printed fabrics. One of her guests also made some beautiful platters of sawn wood to place on the runners. Along the runner we placed some shaped vases, jam jars and also some glass candlesticks with a variety of different flowers in each vase. Votives with a printed pattern matched the fabric tops on the homemade jam favours.

Above Clare, on the arm of her father and followed by her sister, enters the church full of anticipation and excitement.

Opposite The bridal bouquet of 'Shirley Temple' peonies, peach and cream sweet peas, *Astilbe* 'Washington', *Daucus carota*, Peach Avalanche+ and Pearl Avalanche+ spray roses, David Austin's Juliet rose and dusty miller.

Zinc pew ends

To fit with our vintage feel, I suggested zinc balcony pots as pew ends. These pots come with a perfect hook for pews and look great with plants in as well. They are an inexpensive and simple way to decorate the pews if you are doing some of the floral decorations yourself.

INGREDIENTS

mixed foliage (see step 2)

10 bunches of mixed dahlias

an assortment of 50 garden roses

50 stems of white veronica

10 bunches of *Helichrysum* (straw flowers)

10 balcony buckets

green floral foam

1 As these buckets were quite deep and the flowers quite short I decided to use a small amount of foam so the buckets would not be too heavy. Soak the foam in water with flower food for about ten minutes until the bubbles cease to rise in the water.

2 I always like to use three types of foliage to give a natural look, but when the brief is very natural I use at least five different types: thlaspi for its wispy nature, dusty miller for its colour and shaped leaf, snowberries for colour and texture, ivy berries for texture and their classy dark green leaves and rosehips for colour and interest.

3 Once you have covered the foam with foliage and established the shape, you are then ready to add the flowers. Work with the strongest stems first and place more delicate plant material at the end.

Rose petal confetti

Natural confetti is increasingly popular for its fragrance and for its green credentials. Many vicars, particularly in urban areas, are not keen on the littering effect of paper confetti, so this is the answer.

INGREDIENTS

mixed rose petals

some squares of reasonably robust pretty paper

a small stapler

a display basket with rigid high sides

a length of ribbon

1 First wrap the paper to make a tightly pointed cone.

2 Staple the overlap to secure the cone.

3 Fill each cone with petals, then place them in the basket. Decorate the handle of the basket with ribbon and a bow.

It is deceptive how many flowers and vessels you need to create this effect.
A variety of heights and shapes of vases works best for this look. Some loose
and longer flowers such as eustoma, veronica, sweet pea and gloriosa work
well in bottles and thin vases, leaving dense heads of hydrangea or groups
of roses for the lower vases. Spread the colour evenly throughout the table.
Arranging them to look visually pleasing is like choreography.

Opposite, clockwise from top left Glass jars were marbled with paint or covered with short lengths of lavender pressed onto double-sided tape and then secured with twine. Posies of hydrangea, rosemary, thlaspi and rosehips surround the Order of Service.

Champagne flutes ready to be charged are edged with jars covered with lavender and filled with rosemary, dill, scabious and gypsophila.

An antique wire bottle holder holds marbled painted bottles and jars filled with roses, rosehips and *Gloriosa superba* 'Red Stripe'.

Along this side of the table are jars of 'Diana's Memory' dahlias, Peach Avalanche+ spray roses, dusty miller, gypsophila and scabious.

Right A branch of cotoneaster was secured into some wet sand and decorated with *Gloriosa superba* 'Red Stripe' to make a wish tree. Guests were invited to write their message for the bride and groom on a postage label and then attach it to the branches.

I prefer to use vases or jars of varying heights with a multitude of flower shapes. Remember lighting candles and votives takes time. Allocate the job to guests if your caterers do not take care of it.

Hessian table runners with
beautiful blocks of wood
laid over them were the base
for the flowers, candles, votives,
fouvours and fruits.

Herb and flower cake topper

One of the inspirations for this wedding was acorns, which are only around for a fleeting few weeks and I had been sizing up my local oak trees on dog walks waiting for the right moment to pick and save some acorns for Clare and Tom's big day. Tom had also been looking out on his parents' farm so that we could have a few at least on the cake. You can see these acorns wired together in a little garland around the bottom tier of the cake. With weddings, often the things I get most stressed about are the things that most guests would not notice or have a clue about! From the point of view of being a floral designer and working with seasonal and often very frail and short-lived plant material I wholeheartedly agree with Mies van der Rohe: 'God is in the details!' Like most things at this wedding, there was a teamwork involved and the mother of the bride made this three-tiered cake. We simply placed flower heads around the base and they are not in foam. Often we start this with some ivies and/or trailing greenery and then lay flowers onto the table.

INGREDIENTS

some herbs and foliage

a selection of small and light flowers

a plastic or polystyrene drinking cup

quarter of a block of floral foam

1 Cut the top off a cup to make a small container for your foam. Next cut some soaked floral foam so it fits snuggly into the bottom of the cup. Make sure the foam is twice as high as the container so you can place plant materials at right angles and conceal the container.

2 First arrange the foliage into a lovely round shape. Use different types of foliage and include some small delicate and frothy varieties – *Alchemilla mollis* is perfect.

3 Add your flowers, starting with the woody and strong stems and moving onto those with frail stems, such as sweet peas.

Opposite The cake garland includes ivies and acorns with 'Shirley Temple' peonies, peach sweet peas, *Astilbe* 'Washington', cream sweet peas, hydrangea, Peach Avalanche+ and Pearl Avalanche+ spray roses, David Austin's Juliet rose and *Gloriosa superba* 'Red Stripe'.

Hot
Pink
Shades

THIS WEDDING THEME marries my favourite colour with some of my favourite wedding flowers: ranunculus, camellia and roses. Recently there has been a trend to take a colour and use shades from either end of the colour spectrum.

'Ombré'-style weddings have long been popular in the US and there are now lots of ombré Pinterest boards to inspire brides. The wedding press also likes the ombré trend as it is very photogenic, and so it has helped to promote this look. In my opinion the ombré trend is best seen in the colour pink, as the range within pink is immense. At one level pink is soft and delicate and at the other end of the scale it is loud and arresting. Roses, ranunculus and gerberas all come in an astonishing range of pinks so they are perfect flowers to use for this effect.

Opposite At one time garden roses were very seasonal but now, thanks to huge production in Kenya and also South America, brides can have this look any time of the year. These Baronesse roses were grown in Colombia in the shade of the Andes, where rose-growing conditions are perfect. These delicate, medium-sized open roses are perfect for wiring into a small shower bouquet with a touch of ivy and *Viburnum tinus* flowering foliage.

Lily, an Italian spinone, with grosgrain lead and bell-shaped floral corsage. Dogs are surprisingly tolerant of floral decorations, though I did turn up at one marquee wedding with a floral collar and as I drove into the drive, I saw the dog making its way down the road. It had grown tired of the disruption at home and decided to head off for some action elsewhere!

Opposite The ombré effect, from light to hot pink, works particularly well with petals. Candlelight – whatever time of day – always adds to ambience.

Towers of roses are a good way to frame the centre of attention on the bride and groom. A long, low and neat arrangement is perfect for the centre of the celebrant's table.

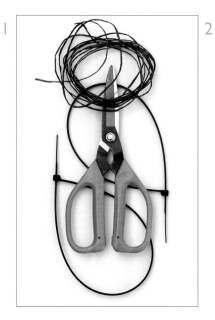

Rose tower

For any event, a few large arrangements will make far more impact than lots of smaller arrangements. To make any flower arrangement of scale the most important thing is to get the mechanics of the arrangement well constructed so that the flowers are secure and not a hazard to guests. I chose three roses in contrasting shades of pink to continue the ombré theme.

INGREDIENTS

12 bunches of camellia foliage

12 bunches of ivy berries

12 bunches of flowering *Viburnum tinus*

80 each of Hot Shot, Acqua! and Sweet Avalanche+ roses

cable ties

cement

3.5-m (12-foot) silver birch pole

large plastic bucket

large urn sprayed silver

10 large floral foam cages

1 Cable ties in all sizes are essential to the event florist – they are strong and versatile.

2 To create the framework for the tower, cement a long, strong silver birch pole into a black plastic flower bucket and then place it into the urn. Next, attach the floral foam cages. The plastic cages contain chamfered blocks of floral foam, which need to be soaked for ten minutes before attaching with cable ties to the birch pole.

3 Green up the cages, moving around the pole so that the foliage comes from all angles and looks rounded.

4 The greenery should completely conceal the foam and cages before you add the roses.

5 Add the flowers using one colour at a time to keep the distribution of colour even.

6 When all three types of rose have been added the colour should balance and the tower is complete.

Previous pages The evening wedding reception was held at Gaynes Park, Essex, with the barn decorated for the event with candles and pink paper honeycomb balls.

The ombré effect was continued into the venue for the evening reception, which had a combination of a traditional linear top table for the bridal party and smaller round tables for the rest of the guests. Clear glass is modern, clean and elegant. The shapes can be matched to the table shape. These low rectangular tanks are wonderful for laying along long tables and great for a top table, so that the bride and groom and the close family are visible to the rest of the room.

On the round tables, glass-stemmed bowls made striking table centres – the grand but simple arrangements included just 20 roses. Ideally, I prefer the table centres this low to allow the guests to communicate more and see around the room. Tall table arrangements can be very dramatic and some locations benefit from a little more height in the floral decoration, but this was not the case here.

Above Here I used the Germini type of gerbera, as the smaller heads were perfect for the holes in the long low vases. They overlap enough for the colours to merge without crowding each other. Having a single flower type in an arrangement uses the colour-shading technique to arresting effect.

Opposite To line the round bowls, first curl some willow stems around the edge. Work from the bottom to the top, pressing it down tightly. When you are happy with the look of the willow, fill the vase with water mixed with flower food. Next make a grid with clear tape across the top of the vase to support the flowers. Add three differently coloured roses in different rotations to mix the colours as much as possible. These are Sweet Avalanche+, Acqua! and Hot Shot.

High Country

Opposite A tiered candelabra is used to decorate the church either side of the altar.

THIS RELAXED COUNTRY MARQUEE WEDDING included a lot of my favourite summer flowers. The inspiration for the colours came from the borders of the garden where the marquee was to be sited. My clients were loyal customers so I was allowed a little more free rein on the flower choices, but one request was that the designs should all feature succulents in one way or another.

Right The marquee is decorated with succulent baskets filled with summer flowers surrounded by green votive lights.

Below Pink and burgundy were used for the wedding flowers to match the sashes of the smaller bridesmaids and the gentlemen's attire. The posy contains 'Sarah Bernhardt' peonies, succulents, flowering mint, 'Black Satin' dahlias, pink sweet peas and *Alchemilla mollis*.

Succulents have been having a renaissance of interest mainly thanks to Pinterest and international wedding blogs. One reason that they deserve to be popular is that they are very attractive and they are nearly indestructible. You can even remove their root for a wedding bouquet and they will later root and continue to flourish. This means they are perfect for recycling! It has also meant that as they are very undemanding plants they have been considered a great choice for a wedding favour.

Succulents are always in style but their popularity has spiked. Technically, a succulent is any plant with fat leaves that means that it can retain water in its fleshy leaves and survive. It is a vast and diverse group of plants and with an enormous variation in colour and habit. For this wedding I used succulents from the *Sempervivum* or *Echeveria* genera.

When I am aiming for a natural country look for a wedding design, I will always use more foliage. I love trailing foliages such as ivy or jasmine and I also like the scent and colours of eucalyptus. *Achemilla mollis* is such a lively green that it makes any colour combination brighter. Foliage is the backdrop for the flowers but it also helps the colours coordinate and creates structure. You get a very different feel when using foliage than if you do not include any. For a tighter, more urban look see Bright Glamour on pages 146–57, where the use of foliage is more restrained.

Opposite The bridal bouquet included pale pink 'Faith' roses, Burgundy Ice and Bridal Piano garden spray roses, 'Maiden's Blush' lilac, eucalyptus, jasmine and *Astrantia major* 'Ruby Wedding'.

Floral foam pew decorations

If you want to make the pew ends ahead of time or you are getting married in a hot climate then the use of a small amount of floral foam will be required. There are several floral foam products on the market to help you achieve this.

Above St Mary's Church in Dalham in Suffolk, decorated in August for a summer wedding.

INGREDIENTS

5 stems of trailing clematis

10 stems of *Alchemilla mollis*

a branch of ivy greenery

15 assorted dahlias

5 'Sarah Bernhardt' peonies

8 Oasis Bioline Mini Florette floral foams

a roll of ribbon

1 The important thing to ascertain before you begin to decide on your pew decorations is how you will hang and display the flowers. Some pew ends are straight and require an S hook or attachment. If you require a clip or hook you may have to use a floral foam product produced by the Smithers Oasis company known as 'Le Klip', or for more delicate pew ends 'Le Petite Klip'. As these pews were diamond shaped I knew I could attach ribbon to them and hang the Mini Florette, which I prefer to Le Klip as it can hold more flowers.

2 After you have soaked your foam in water with flower food for ten minutes you are ready to add your greenery. Choose some to trail, some to cover the foam and some to add a fluffy and vibrant look. You are aiming for a diamond shape in outline, profile and depth. Aim for height in the middle of the diamond.

3 Add dahlias so that you create a zig-zag across the arrangement from top to bottom. Next add the focal peonies so that they have the best position in the arrangement. The central flower will set the highest point of the profile of the decoration.

4 Continue to add the other coloured dahlias. Loop a metre of ribbon through the hole in the handle of the plastic Mini Florette and you are ready to hang it onto the pew.

For long oval tables, succulents were wired into the baskets to create a more sculptural effect. Astrantia, garden roses, sweet peas, *Alchemilla mollis*, mint and clematis were added to the centrepieces. The coordinating table linen, napkins, chairs, glassware and crockery make the wedding breakfast unique.

Succulent basket

One of my signature looks is to adapt a container to make it appear more sculptural. I am always on the lookout for more interesting baskets or containers that can be given a natural makeover.

These baskets are handmade for me in Spain by artisan basketmakers in San José. Any loose weave but sturdy baskets will do. This chicken wire is a feature of a lot of metal kitchen baskets in Europe, particularly in France, so look out for those, too.

Below I have always adored succulents, whose fleshy leaves have adapted to hold more moisture. This means that they are very graphic with a pronounced profile. From Seoul to Boston, where this trend started, these plants are the A-list guest at your wedding.

INGREDIENTS

15 *Tillandsia xerographica* (air plants)

10 stems of *Eucalyptus pulverulenta* 'Baby Blue'

10 succulent plants or stems of echeveria varieties

10 stems of *Astrantia major* var. *rosea*

10 stems of *Viburnum opulus* 'Roseum'

10 stems of 'Mona Lisa Deep Blue' anemones

10 Faith roses

10 Cool Water roses

10 *Eustoma* 'Kyoto Purple'

3 stems of vanda orchids

a bundle of 1.00mm (18 gauge) wires

sturdy basket

plastic pot

a length of 5-cm (2-inch) chicken wire

a handful of carpet moss

1 First you need to attach the succulents and air plants to the wires. For the air plants, push a wire through the stem horizontally. Then bring both ends down in the same direction as the stem and twist one wire over the stem three times to create a double-leg mount to attach to the basket. Wire the stems of eucalyptus in the same way. Use the same method for the succulents, but they will also need a wire up through the centre of the stem to anchor them, as they are heavier.

2 Attach the wired succulents and air plants around the sides of the basket, using the eucalyptus to fill any gaps. When the basket is completed, place a plastic container inside it. Next scrunch up a length of chicken wire and push it into the container, making sure the wire is proud of the edge of the container and the basket. Secure the container in the basket with moss and fill with water mixed with flower food. Wire three succulents, two air plants and some eucalyptus into the chicken wire to establish your structure.

3 Start to add your flowers, using the softer flowers first. Small dainty flowers need to be added in groups to look balanced with the large flower heads.

4 To finish off, cut the three stems of vanda orchids into two or three sections so that you can place them in key positions around the design.

Left Fringed tulips are my favourite tulips and this white 'Honeymoon' variety has to be one of the best. They look stunning with lace or sheer dresses.

Opposite My favourite flower to use with a black and white theme is the black-eyed anemone. Be sure to ask for the 'Black-eyed Beauty' variety as some white anemones have green centres. They have been used here with white 'Carnegie' hyacinths for scent and also 'Honeymoon' tulips.

Black is the New White

ORIGINALLY PEOPLE WHO CHOSE BLACK as a theme for their weddings were out to shock! They wanted something edgy, untraditional and almost anti-wedding in feel. It was a protest against the princess dresses, fairy-tale locations and all the pomp and ceremony that go with the image of a traditional white wedding.

Then about ten years ago, black and white weddings became the mark of high sophistication. Hankering after the feel of a former age and time, black and white weddings were seen as classical and smart. Black and white is timeless and, on film, very flattering. The absence of colour is seductive. It conjures up iconic images of the yesteryear weddings of Grace Kelly and Jackie Onassis. Inspired by Hollywood glamour and actresses such as Audrey Hepburn and Marilyn Monroe, the black and white wedding is very alluring and elegant.

In the absence of colour, texture and shape become more important and make the black and white wedding very classical. It works well for both lavish weddings or very intimate celebrations. It is definitely a more formal style than informal, and I think if you do want a more informal wedding it is best to choose another theme, as the casual black and white look can end up looking rather more gothic than glamorous! Keep the details to a minimum to achieve style and sophistication. If you want to make your black and white wedding more Art Deco, then accents of silver and gold will enhance.

A good all-year-round choice of a white flower with a black centre is a gerbera daisy. These come in two sizes and the small germini would be perfect for buttonholes. Often brides and grooms who are planning a more sophisticated black and white wedding will be attracted to roses or calla lilies. Both of these have burgundy and almost black varieties, to contrast with the white varieties.

The choice for white flowers is easy but black flowers are harder. In truth, there are no really black flowers, and even if you used dyed flowers they are more aubergine than true black. The nearest you can get to black flowers are the very darkest shades of purple or red. All the hybridizers and flower growers in the world would love to produce a black flower and it is certainly the holy grail for breeders. The first seasonal black flowers of the year are the 'Queen of Night' tulips, which create moody displays. I like the contrast of black flowers with grey foliage rather than green, and there are lots of black berries that can be incorporated into designs from autumn to spring. Blackberries, *Ligustrum* and *Viburnum tinus* are three of my favourites. In summer look out for black cornflowers or black dahlias to add seasonal colour.

Above left The black centres of anemones are very intricate and interesting because they have beautifully detailed stamens and pistils. The petals are papery and very delicate.

Above A small sprig of foliage or a few leaves are usually used to accompany a buttonhole. White heather has long been associated with good fortune and good luck, and so both the rose and the anemone have had a small sprig attached for luck.

Opposite The bridesmaid carries a posy of white serrated-edged 'Honeymoon' tulips and *Anemone coronaria* 'Galil Wit'.

Black and white has a very timeless quality and so I think as a wedding theme choice it will stand the test of time. It suits urban venues very well and looks smart in formal locations. I think it works particularly well in Art Deco hotels such as Claridges in London or the Waldorf-Astoria in New York. Often clients also want to add another accent colour to the mix, but personally I think it works best when kept simple, and it looks strongest if the white and black are separated as seen here.

Opposite Here black Danish taper candles and black votives have been used to create ambiance. The black ribbon detail that was used on the invitation also appears around the table centres, the cake and the napkins.

Above A simple three-tiered cake by the Little Venice Cake Company has been decorated with a small posy of 'Pauline Violet' ranunculus. Interestingly, the top search on the internet for black and white weddings is for the black and white cake!

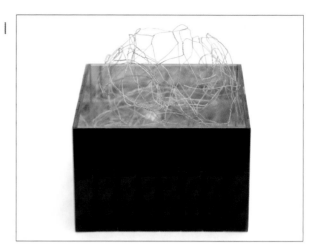

I

White and black centrepiece

All-white flowers in black containers look very smart. I love to include some scent in all my wedding schemes and freesias, hyacinths and lilac are my fragrance notes for this wedding. Scent is so evocative and is a very powerful memory of the day.

INGREDIENTS

10 stems of *Brachyglottis* 'Sunshine'

10 stems of *Ruscus hypophyllum*

10 short *Viburnum opulus* 'Roseum'

10 stems of white lilac

20 Avalanche+ roses

10 white *Hyacinthus orientalis* 'Carnegie'

20 'Honeymoon' tulips

30 white 'Argenta' freesias

a length of 5-cm (2-inch) chicken wire

a black mirror rectangular vase

double-sided tape

a length of ribbon

2

3

I Crunch a length of chicken wire into the vase. Make sure it fits snugly and rises above the edge of the container. For this design I chose to use wire rather than foam because many of the spring flowers have fleshy or fragile stems and they are thirsty drinkers. They will last better and look more vigorous arranged in water mixed with flower food.

2 Attach the ribbon around the vase with double-sided tape. Arrange the foliage first to create the shape and height you want the arrangement to be, and to create a base for the flowers. All the stems should radiate from the centre.

3 Add the woody-stemmed *Viburnum opulus* throughout the design and then add the woody-stemmed lilac and roses. This will make a good structure to hold the fleshy-stemmed hyacinths and tulips and the more delicate freesias in place.

Trimming vases with ribbon is an easy
way to customize a simple container.
I particularly like to use grosgrain or
velvet ribbon for this task.

Glowing
Garden

OUTDOOR CELEBRATIONS in the UK always require a wet and
a dry weather plan and their rarity makes them even more
special. On this occasion we had the most amazing sunny day
in July, but the sun was so fierce it meant we had to keep the
flowers under the shade of trees until the last minute. This
required some last minute adrenaline and all hands on decks!
The theme of this wedding was to use hot colours and include
some fruits. The hosts also wanted to make the most of the
abundant seasonal flowers available in mid-summer.

Opposite An ancient mulberry tree became a feature for this
garden reception, when the base was planted with flowering
plants and decorated with hanging and pole votives.

Opposite In keeping with the brightly colourful theme, the bride's bouquet contained 'Sarah Bernhardt' peonies, bright pink 'Tenga-Venga' and orange Milva spray roses, *Alchemilla mollis*, *Asclepias tuberosa*, *Gloriosa superba* 'Rothschildiana' and quaking grass.

My personal inspiration for brightly coloured flower schemes often comes from the colours of India, Morocco and Mexico. Bright colours suit hot weather as bright sun can bleach colours, and I adore experimenting with the combination of pink and orange. Usually I use hot pinks to balance with the orange, but as this wedding was in the middle of the peony season we also added some softer pinks. It is also important to make the arrangements more intense by adding some lime green, and so the seasonal quaking grass, *Chasmanthium latifolium*, *Alchemilla mollis* and *Anethum graveolens* were used throughout. *Gloriosa superba* 'Rothschildiana' is then perfect for pulling the pink and the lime green together, and the rarity of this flower always draws attention.

Food stations and bars were arranged around the garden, and this gave me the opportunity to use lots of vertical tiers of flowers on metal stands. We also agreed to do some large installations of flowers that would grab the attention of the guests as they made their way into the garden.

Above Silk votive holders have been filled with eupatorium and brightly coloured Germini gerberas for the bridesmaids to carry.

Left This beautiful garden in Cambridge had enough trees with low horizontal branches to add masses of silk votives. Fruit trees are good for this decoration; some trees are just too grand, tall and old for this to work successfully.

Left A floral chandelier was created to fill the roof of the gazebo by wiring together contorted willow and then adding some hanging vases filled with pink, orange and green flowers. Pea lights were added to many trees and garden features to create a twinkling effect as the sun went down.

Right Metal-tiered stands held glass vases and votives. The splash of pink and orange from the scattered cushions brightens dark or green corners of the garden.

Opposite above right The table posies included peonies, Purple Power roses, 'Babe' spray roses, *Carthamus* 'Zanzibar', *Anethum graveolens* and orange *Gloriosa* 'Leonella'.

Opposite below right Three-tiered stand of terracotta pots filled with *Alchemilla mollis*, *Carthamus* 'Zanzibar', *Asclepias tuberosa*, Cherry-O! roses and 'Babe' spray roses and featuring 'Sarah Bernhardt' peonies.

Structured bar arrangement

I love tall vases on bars where room is tight, and this design is both striking and economical on space. My impromptu purchase for this wedding was some gorgeous pink bougainvillea plants that we cut to use in this bar design. The other plants we used to brighten existing pots in the garden. Grouping flowers makes the colour more dramatic and seemed perfect for this statement piece. Even if you are using a ceramic or coloured glass vase, you have to be careful that the bottom of the floral foam ball does not make a mess in the vase and so we usually make sure that the bottom of the foam is covered in plastic film to prevent unsightly debris or dirty water appearing in the vase.

Left A 20-cm (8-inch) ball of floral foam was used to create a colourful ball of flowers in groups of orange, pink and lime green.

Opposite Although both bar designs have the same colour combination, you can see how the green foliage dilutes the overall effect in comparison to the grouped arrangement. Pink and orange accessories were used throughout to add further splashes of bright colour.

Unstructured bar arrangement

In contrast, this large metal pumpkin makes a great organic-shaped container for a loose and natural arrangement of flowers using the same colour palette.

INGREDIENTS

10 stems of *Molucella laevis*

10 stems of cotinus

1 bunch of copper beech (*Fagus sylvatica*)

10 stems of *Eucalyptus pulverulenta* 'Baby Blue'

10 stems of *Antirrhinum majus* 'Monaco Rose'

10 'Sarah Bernhardt' peonies

10 'Kansas' peonies

10 stems of stephanandra

10 stems of *Carthamus tinctorious* 'Zanzibar'

10 stems of *Celosia cristata* 'Persimmon Chief'

10 stems of *Gloriosa rothschildiana*

large round container

1 Fill the container with water and flower food. A good mixture of foliage makes the structure for this flower design. I used different-shaped plant materials for the base: pointed molucella for height and structure, bushy smoke-bush cotinus to fill out and burgundy beech for colour.

2 Once you have established the shape and outline of the arrangement, begin to add the flowers. Usually I start with the tall or spire flowers such as the antirrhinum, move on to the more focal flower such as the peonies, and then use the fillers, such as the carthamus.

3 Delicate stems such as the gloriosa are left to the end so they are not damaged when you insert other stems. Make sure some flowers and foliage hang down over the container for a rounded, natural shape.

Orange and peony tower

The construction of this tower is the same as the one shown on page 99. A birch tree stem was set into a bucket with some cement. Floral foam cages were then placed on either side of the pole. As we were using a lot of oranges in this design, we also added some chicken wire to hold everything tightly into place around the column. After the mechanics are organized, the foliage is added to make a thick column of greenery. With large arrangements where we require a ladder we often work in twos so that one person can hand material for the other to arrange.

INGREDIENTS

a catering box of oranges

20 bunches of salal (*Gaultheria shallon*)

100 stems of *Hypericum* Magical Dream

100 Wow roses

60 Pink Piano roses

60 Purple Power roses

100 'Sarah Bernhardt' peonies

60 stems of *Celosia* 'Bombay Candy'

40 stems of *Celosia* 'Bombay Firosa'

100 stems of *Alchemilla mollis*

100 stems of *Anethum graveolens*

100 *Nectaroscordum siculum* flowers

100 stems of poppy seed heads

3.5-m (12-foot) silver birch pole set in cement in a large plastic bucket, placed in an urn and covered with 10 floral foam cages (see page 99 step 2)

2.5-cm (1-inch) chicken wire

30-cm (12-inch) bamboo skewers

1 Push the bamboo skewers firmly into the oranges, but without coming right through.

2 Cover the frame with the foliage to give it a lovely fluffy effect. Then position the oranges evenly over the design by pushing the skewers into the foam. The oranges add colour and texture.

3 Once the oranges are evenly spaced, add the focal flowers – starting with the roses. You need to stand back occasionally to see how the overall effect is looking. When working so close to such a huge structure it is hard to see how the design is progressing.

4 Then add the peonies and celosia evenly all over the tower. I also chose to use some scented alliums. *Nectaroscordum siculum* is one of my favourite of the ornamental onion family. It has bell-shaped creamy green flowers fluxed with red and lilac. Also known as the Sicilian honey lily, it has a curious sweet garlic and honey fragrance. Add the poppy seed heads.

5 Finally, add the *Alchemilla mollis* and green dill among the flowers and oranges to fill any gaps.

Above The towers of peonies and oranges flank a gelato picnic spot set up in the garden for wedding guests to enjoy.

Opposite When you are decorating an outdoor area you need to make some impact with your arrangements.

1

2

3

4

5

Left The classical and elegant interior of St Mary-le-Bow Church in the City of London. Pew ends and urns of flowers flank the central aisle ready for the bride's entrance.

Summer in the City

Opposite Cornflowers and hydrangeas were the muse flowers for this blue-themed summer City wedding. Two rings including these key flowers were placed on the entrance doors of the church to welcome the guests.

THE MAJESTIC CHURCH of St Mary-le-Bow on Cheapside in the City of London has had a very lively history. This famous church was founded in 1080 but burnt down in the Great Fire of London in 1666. Rebuilt by Sir Christopher Wren, it was destroyed once more in the Second World War in 1941. It was rebuilt again and reconsecrated in 1964. The church occupies a central position in the old City of London and so the areas where you could hear the bells were historically within the city wall boundary. Therefore people who were born with the sounds of these bells were considered real Londoners and were considered Cockneys. My bride and groom, who live and work in London, decided on a City wedding. They chose this church because of family associations with the Worshipful Company of Cordwainers, the professional shoemakers who historically lived in this area of London and who have ancient connections with this church.

I first met the bride and groom through one of my former floral designers, who is now living overseas. She had already suggested some ideas and flowers to the bride, and so they came to me knowing they wanted their flowers to be predominantly blue and white to match their bridesmaids's dresses, and also that they wanted to have cornflowers for their buttonholes. The fine church also has a lovely sky-blue ceiling. Over a few meetings – and a change of reception venue – the design was agreed. Pink was added to one of the bridesmaid's bouquets, and it was also agreed to add a little more colour to the palette of the flowers at the reception.

Opposite Pinning buttonholes onto the ushers and Philip the groom outside St Mary-Le-Bow in Cheapside. The all-blue buttonholes of cornflower, lavender and pistachio foliage were for the men, while the ladies also had three white 'Snowflake' rosebuds.

Above The bride Kathryn and her maids take a break for photographs between the church ceremony and the reception. Hydrangeas in different colours make simple but stunning round bouquets.

The City of London makes a lovely historic backdrop for a wedding. There are lots of wonderful churches in the City and also lots of great entertaining spaces. Many old banking halls have been transformed into modern restaurants and venues. The square mile of the City is often deserted at the weekend and it is very accessible. The bride and groom chose this venue when a change of ownership altered their plans for another venue. The reception was held in an old banking hall in Lombard Street. Charles Dickens' first love Maria Beadnell's father was the manager of the bank and the young Dickens would walk to Lombard Street to gaze upon the place where Maria lived. The venue had some round banqueting tables that were 1.5m (5 feet) in diameter, but they also used some of the restaurant banquette seating, which left little room for flower arrangements. These had to be narrow and not too long.

A tied pew end of blue hydrangea, sage, *Viburnum opulus*, white snowberries, white veronica, 'Avalanche' roses and astrantia.

This handsome church has two pulpits and so we decorated them with a central spray of flowers. Different ivies, rosemary, eucalyptus and mint are the background foliages for hydrangea, scabious, veronica and Avalanche+ roses.

Late summer pedestal

In late summer you have plenty of long-stemmed plant material to choose from – perfect for creating really impressive large-scale pedestal arrangements to decorate the venue for your reception.

INGREDIENTS

15 stems of tall arching stephanandra

2 bunches of long eucalyptus

3 bunches of tall forsythia foliage

10 stems of tall *Cotinus coggygria* 'Royal Purple'

10 stems of *Delphinium* 'Delphi's Secret'

10 stems of *Delphinium* 'Alis Duyvenstein'

10 stems of *Delphinium* 'Blue Star'

5 *Gentiana* 'Ashiro-no-aki'

5 *Hydrangea macrophylla* 'Verena Classic'

5 *Hydrangea macrophylla* 'Rodea Paars Classic'

7 'Helvetia' Oriental lilies

large plastic bucket

urn

a length of 5-cm (2-inch) chicken wire

a reel of florist's wire

1 Secure a plastic bucket into the urn and fill with a ball of chicken wire to provide a support for the foliage and flowers. Secure the chicken wire with a tape of wire so that it is firm.

2 Taking the tallest foliage first, fill the urn so that all the stems are radiating from the central point of the bucket. Use arching stems of the stephanandra to soften the edge of the urn so the overall shape of the plant material is rounded.

3 Add the purple cotinus – this makes the colour combination richer. Continue to fill the urn with all your foliage so that you make a firm base for your flowers.

4 Start with the tall delphiniums and gentians and then add the hydrangeas around the sides of the arrangement. Fill the gaps with the Oriental lilies.

A mixture of flower shapes are best for pedestal arrangements, with some tall spires such as delphinium, some star-shaped lilies and some round flowers such as hydrangea.

1

2

3

4

Door wreath

Some form of decoration at the entrance to your ceremony venue sets the tone for the wedding flowers. These hydrangea rings pick up on the flower choices for the bridal and bridesmaids' bouquets and establish the colour theme.

INGREDIENTS

a bunch of galax leaves

10 stems of *Alchemilla mollis*

5 stems of *Viburnum tinus*

5 stems of snowberries

5 stems of white dill

3 hybrid hydrangeas

1 bunch of blue autumnal garden hydrangea

7 white Avalanche+ roses

5 agapanthus

a bunch of brodiaea

30-cm (12-inch) floral foam ring

a length of blue ribbon

1 Soak the foam ring and tie the ribbon around the frame.

2 Edge the wreath with galax leaves to hide the polystyrene back. Start to build up the ring using different foliage. Place the plant material at different angles to make it look rounded.

3 Use some *Alchemilla mollis* and viburnum to create some height and movement to the wreath.

4 Start placing the hybrid hydrangeas in key areas of the frame and then fill with the garden hydrangea. Place the roses so that they face in different directions and levels throughout the circle. Fill with the remaining flowers.

This venue had some round tables and some thin long tables with banquet seating. For the round banqueting tables we covered pots with white heather and filled them with pistachio foliage, hydrangea, snowberry, and Avalanche+ roses.

Above left A hand-tied posy of hydrangeas, Sweet Avalanche+roses and blue veronica in a blue glass container.

Above Square glass containers were filled with English seasonal hydrangeas just beginning to turn autumnal, echinops, *Daucus carota* 'Dara', Sweet Avalanche+ standard roses and Avalanche+ spray roses mixed with eustoma.

Left Pink hydrangea and Sweet Avalanche+ roses in a blue glass fishbowl with scented mint and gorgeous pink snowberries (*Symphoricarpos* Charming Fantasy).

Above right Framed by a dramatic domed skylight, this smart City restaurant was located close to St Mary-le-Bow church and so the guests could easily walk from the service to the reception. No 1 Lombard Street used to be a banking hall so it has great proportions.

Below right As some of the tables were long and thin with banquette seating, we filled small glass boats with hydrangeas and then added pistachio foliage, echinops, flowering mint, scabious, cornflower, *Alchemilla mollis*, Vendela roses and the white dahlia 'Karma Maarten Zwaan'.

Bright
Glamour

THE CHOICE OF VENUE can often dictate the kind of style
your wedding will exude, and a blank canvas such as a white
space or a marquee gives you freedom to express yourself.
The bride and groom at this wedding wanted to have the
ceremony and party in one venue so it would be easy for
all the guests. They wanted a London location and the
emphasis was on the party, with a club feel. The OXO2, a
white gallery and event space on the River Thames below
the famous Oxo Tower restaurant, is the perfect venue.
This iconic building and chic event space provided enough
space for them to hold their civil ceremony, enjoy drinks
and the wedding breakfast at their leisure before dancing
well into the night.

Brightly coloured mixed roses became the flower theme,
and fuchsia pink our accent colour for the bridesmaids'
dresses and also the table linen. As the space has high
ceilings we settled upon tall, flared glass vases filled with
balls of roses and *Viburnum opulus* for all the tables.

Right Stars of the show, the roses (from top to bottom) are
All 4 Love+, Marie-Claire!, Ocean Song, Memory Lane and Purple
Power, here backed with magnolia buds and *Viburnum opulus*.

Opposite Tall vases – both on the tables and floor standing – and
chair backs include multicoloured roses, camellia and ivy berry
foliage and lime-green balls of *Viburnum opulus*.

146

Ten floor-standing candelabras line the aisle, with chair backs adorning the back row of guest chairs. White plinths and curvy vases have been filled with a dome of mixed coloured roses and branches of magnolia for dramatic effect.

I found the floor-standing candlesticks in Paris at the Maison et Objet fair, where I often go on buying trips for unusual and original accessories. They were originally made in Scandinavia, and look especially good with Danish taper candles. Bold colours have impact in a white room and I always prefer to leave out white in the floral decorations as this distracts the eye. For this wedding we decided to use elegantly shaped white glass vases to accentuate the colour of the roses on fuchsia pink linen. Coloured candles were chosen to stand out against the white walls, and we all liked the Danish taper candles made by chandlers Ester and Eric Meller. They began their candle business around the same time I started my flower business. These drip-less candles are wonderful for events and of course I adore their colour range. If you are using candles in either your reception or ceremony venue, to avoid drips and smoke make sure that the wick is 1cm (1/3 inch) long and the candles are kept out of the way of draughts or air-conditioning. And always check beforehand that your venue allows the use of candles – many historic buildings don't.

While the guests sat down to the wedding breakfast, the ceremony area was transformed into a nightclub with Chesterfield sofas and low seating areas. Hundreds of votives were added to make the venue sparkle and reflect all the night-time lights on the River Thames below.

Rosalind Miller made this elegant four-tiered wedding cake, and we added a rose plinth to the base and also a rose dome to match the table arrangements. The ribbon trim matches the colour of the table linen.

Rose chair backs

Chair backs are a neat way to line an aisle for a ceremony or frame the entrance. The knack to get a good-looking chair back is to have the right foliage to make the outline diamond shaped and the profile triangular. If they are too flat, they don't look as good. Flat-leafed foliages such as salal or camellia are good for the back and then a busy berried or flowering foliage helps to get a good profile.

INGREDIENTS

9 roses – I used 3 Camel, 3 Moody Blues and 3 Riviera

3 stems of camellia foliage

3 stems of ivy berries

3 stems of *Viburnum opulus*

a roll of bind wire or strong string

a length of ribbon

1 Clean the thorns off the roses with a sharp knife and remove the lower foliage from the greenery and roses.

2 Placing the flat foliage at the back and holding the foliage in your left hand (if you are right-handed) arrange so you are creating a diamond-shaped outline and a triangular-shaped profile.

3 When you have achieved a good shape with the foliage you are ready to start to add the roses and the viburnum, zig-zagging through the centre of the chair back. Leave some smaller and lower pieces of foliage to create a return end at the base, where you will tie the bunch.

4 Tie with bind wire and then make a three-looped ribbon bow to cover the tie (see page 168 steps 6 to 7). Leave enough ribbon to then knot onto the chair.

2

3

4

These tied swags of flowers can be added just before the ceremony. When the room is being changed for the reception, as in this case, we often move them and place them on top-table chairs.

Opposite Used as one of a pair to delineate the area where the bride and groom stood for the wedding service itself, this tall arrangement is of mixed Black Baccara, All 4 Love+, Marie-Claire!, Ocean Song, Purple Power and Cool Water roses studded with ming (or asparagus) fern and *Viburnum opulus* in a dome shape, with branches of magnolia giving height.

Above The round bridesmaid's bouquet contained Combo, All 4 Love+ and Deep Water roses with ivy berries and *Viburnum opulus*.

Above This beautiful laser-cut wedding stationery is from Cutture. The orchid garden menu has been tied around the napkin with grosgrain ribbon. The pink spray rose is Classic Lydia.

FLORAL
DECORATIONS

Bridal
Bouquets

INTERESTINGLY, THE BRIDAL BOUQUET is often the last thing to get decided on. There are two really key points to think about. The first is that the bouquet must suit your personality – and believe me there is a flower for every individual – and secondly it must suit the dress. I have had the pleasure of meeting many couture designers and I know they would always match the flowers to the dress. With luck you have found the perfect dress that suits you and your personal style, and now you need the perfect bouquet to match.

I also advise brides that whatever choice of general theme they have selected for their wedding, it is still more important for the flowers to match the dress. In my opinion, if that means the bouquet does not fit in with the overall look, it is irrelevant. Although it might feel like a theatre production to arrange all the floral decorations, after the event most people retain a simple photo of the bride and the groom, and that usually features the bouquet.

Above A simple and elegant tied bouquet of white calla lilies.

Opposite A traditional cream and white wired shower bouquet of ruscus, jasmine, Quick Sand roses, white double freesias, Snowdance spray roses and the white lilac *Syringa vulgaris* 'Madame Florent Stepman'.

Previous pages, left A traditional mandap is decorated with succulents, *Tillandsia xerographica* air plants, 'Pole Ice' gerberas and the mini gerbera 'Kermit'.
Right Jasmine and white vanda orchids form a simple teardrop bouquet.

An overarm bouquet of Kobe, a lovely large-
headed white phalaenopsis orchid.

A colourful wired shower bouquet of eucalyptus, *Viburnum opulus*, *Gloriosa* 'Rothschildiana', 'Tenga-venga' and 'Blue Curiosa' roses and the vanda orchid 'Kanchana Magic Blue'.

Mini cascade bouquet

INGREDIENTS

10 stems of small-headed white phalaenopsis 'Venice' mini orchids

a roll of bind wire

a roll of gutta percha tape

2m (6 feet) of white ribbon

Phalaenopsis orchids make wonderful flowers to hand tie into a simple but very chic bouquet. In their natural habitat they grow under the forest canopy and are an epiphyte, which means they are naturally air plants and do not need soil to root. Their branched inflorescence flows down and can be as long as a metre, making them perfect for cascading or show bouquets.

1 Arrange the orchids in your hand using the longest ones to make the end of the bouquet first, then building up.

2 Add smaller lengths of the orchids to each side. It is easier if you do this looking into a mirror, so you can see how your bouquet is building up. It is far easier to access the shape this way.

3 When you are happy with the shape, tie at the binding point where you have been holding the bouquet with bind wire. Trim the stems so that the handle is just a bit longer than your fist.

4 Attach the gutta percha tape at the top of the stems and, stretching it out, bind it around the stems so that it covers them all and keeps them bound together.

5 Now take the length of ribbon and bind the ribbon down the stems and back up so that the stems are all covered with ribbon.

6 When you reach the top under the start of the flower heads you can add a three-looped bow as shown on page 168 steps 6 to 7 or tie with a knot.

Opposite A hand-tied cascade of 'Venice' mini phalaenopsis orchids makes an elegant bouquet for a more mature bride or for those planning their second or third wedding. It is light to carry and very sophisticated.

There are no really hard and fast rules about the colours of bridal bouquets and it really is a matter of personal taste. White and cream are still overwhelmingly the most popular, but many brides feel they want to add some colour to the bridal gown. The round bouquet has been the most common in recent times, and very often brides mix white with the colours used in their bridesmaids' bouquets. White works well with shades of blue, pink, peach and cream. It does not work so well with darker colours or mixed colours, as it draws the eye too much.

The one floral accessory that everyone will remember will be your bridal bouquet. You should be able to work with your florist to create a unique bouquet that is perfect for you, suits your dress and that you feel comfortable carrying. It will be the most photographed arrangement on the day. I often get letters from brides after their weddings saying they loved the bouquet so much they did not want to throw it to their guests!

Clockwise from top left 'Kansas' peonies with pale pink 'Europa' astilbe. 'Chiffon Parfait' pale pink peonies with white sweet peas and pale pink 'Europa' astilbe. Peach 'Coral Charm' and pinky peach 'Coral Sunset', dark red 'Red Charm' and pink 'Kansas' peonies in a hand-tied posy.

A sumptuous mixed bridal bouquet of 'Shirley Temple' peonies, *Astilbe* 'Washington', peach 'Misty Champagne' and pink 'Misty Pink' sweet peas, white Avalanche+ spray roses, Pearl Avalanche+ standard roses, *Senecio cineraria* and *Brachyglottis* 'Sunshine'.

Classic hand-tied bouquet

This is still the most popular style for a bridal bouquet. The simplicity of the shape shows off the flowers to perfection, so if you have a favourite bloom you want to use this is the ideal design for you.

INGREDIENTS

30 Bella Rosa or Bellevue roses

a roll of bind wire

a roll of gold organza ribbon

1 Before you begin to make your bouquet it is important to remove all the lower foliage and gently prise off all the thorns from the roses with a knife. Take one central rose about 5cm (2 inches) from the flower head into your left hand. Add the second rose to the right of the central rose at an acute angle of around 12°. Then add another rose and continue until you have added five. Then, using your right hand, twist the bunch 180°.

2 Now you have turned the bunch you are working on the other side. Add a further five roses. Twist again around 90° and repeat. Keep twisting and adding roses, always to the left-hand side of the bunch but changing the angle by turning it around. This becomes instinctual with practice and does not have to be every five flowers.

Opposite A hand-tied posy of Bellevue roses is a classic choice for a bridal bouquet.

3 Carry on building a dome of roses so the final roses to be placed are positioned at more of a right angle. You should not have any leaves in the binding point or on the lower stems. The point at which you have been holding the bunch in your right hand is the area you will bind the bouquet together by tying with a strong wire. I prefer bind wire, which you will need to attach while still holding the flowers.

4 Tie the bouquet together tightly to hold it into place but not so hard as to cut the stems.

5 Trim the stems evenly, leaving a handle a bit longer than your fist.

6 Make an S-shaped loop with the ribbon, pinching it into the middle with your thumb and your first finger. Continue with a second loop and then a third.

7 When you have the three loops that snake through the centre as figure of eights you are ready to cut a further length of ribbon and place it through the centre to attach to the bouquet. Tie the ribbon over the bind wire to conceal it.

'Combo' roses have been made into a Malmaison bouquet. These bouquets are sometimes also referred to as Glamelia bouquets, and they are composite bouquets where individual petals are used to create the final form. Constance Spry was the first to make these bouquets in the mid twentieth century. They also work with orchids, some lilies and ornamental kales, but personally I prefer them made from roses. While they are stunningly beautiful they are delicate, as each petal is individually wired. I would be cautious of suggesting this bouquet for a wedding on a hot day or in a humid climate. They are very time-consuming to make and so are expensive.

Wired bouquets are lighter than hand-tied bouquets and so that is why traditionally wedding bouquets were always wired. This classic white bouquet uses Exclusive Sensation white spray roses with scented stephanotis and white snowberries (*Symphoricarpos* Magical Snowqueen) edged with *Hosta* 'Francee' leaves.

Modern Victorian posy

THE VICTORIAN POSY was first popular in the mid nineteenth century, often backed with lace. Traditionally, concentric circles of pink, blue and lilac flowers would have been wired into a neat round posy.

INGREDIENTS

16 Maritim roses

10 'Hot Pink' ranunculus

50 stems of muscari

3 bunches of variegated lily grass

3 bunches of galax leaves

a roll of bind wire or strong string

a length of ribbon

1 First clean all the plant material really well so there are no thorns on the roses and no lower foliage on the flowers. Look for the straightest rose and then place in your left hand, holding your hand about 2.5cm (1 inch) below the rose sepals.

2 Next take the ranunculus and place the heads around the single rose, but just a little lower to make a small dome. If you are attempting this for the first time you might want to tie at this stage.

3 Take the muscari in bunches of seven stems and add to the posy below the ranunculus at about a 30° angle as shown. Work round the ranunculus until you have a gorgeous thick circle of muscari. Tie again to hold in place.

4 Now you are ready to add the last circle of flowers, placing the roses, again at an angle, a little lower than the muscari. Their round shape helps to give a pronounced dome to the arrangement and also makes it look more symmetrical. Tie again under the roses.

5 Instead of a lace edge I like to make a decorative effect with leaves, and the long variegated blades of lily grass make a lovely swirly effect when twisted and looped around the bunch. Then tie to keep them all in place.

6 Finally add a collar of galax leaves, taking three or so together and moving round the bunch creating a ruffled edge of leaves. The galax leaves make a good return end as they fall back over the binding point. Tie again with bind wire.

7 Cut the stems so they are slightly longer than the width of your hand. Tie the ribbon around the binding point.

I like to make my Victorian
posies without any wires
and I have to say spring is
my preferred season to
make them, with muscari
and ranunculus being two
of my favoured flower
varieties for this design.
The circles represent
eternity and suggest
everlasting love.

Bridesmaids and Flower Girls

THE CHIEF BRIDESMAID and the adult bridesmaids have important roles supporting the bride both leading up to and on the day itself, and looking after the juniors in the bridal party. The child bridesmaids, flower girls and pages generally have an aesthetic role and so you can make the most of your floral decorations to enhance the beauty of your wedding party. Flower girls are usually an addition or an alternative to bridesmaids and their role is usually to scatter petals of lavender or roses down the aisle before the bridal procession, and then join the party after the ceremony in the recessional down the aisle.

Above A circular bridesmaid's headdress of sprigs of rosemary, silver leaves of *Brachyglottis* 'Sunshine', berries, sprigs of white gypsophila and small florets of autumnal hydrangea.

This wild-flower bridesmaid's bouquet includes *Miscanthus sinensis* 'Malepartus', *Alchemilla mollis*, *Craspedia*, *Echinacea purpurea* 'White Swan', *Eryngium* 'Orion Questar', *Dianthus* Giant Gipsy and 'Onesta' and 'New Orange' dahlias.

A talented florist will be able to make you any kind of floral accessory you require for your wedding day. I have made moss teddies, halos and even a cupid's bow and arrow. We have accessorized shoes, handmuffs, handbags and even made a floral scarf. Your florist could make you a pillow of flowers for your ring bearers, fashion you a lucky horseshoe or decorate collars and headdresses for family pets or treasured animals involved in the proceedings. By the careful use of wired flower heads many clever, imaginative and intricate designs can be created to make your wedding truly individual.

Usually, the colours for the bridal party outfits are chosen before the flowers are decided on and invariably it will influence the colours of the flowers. It is customary for each bridesmaid or flower girl to hold some flowers. These could be individual stems, a small posy, a basket or bag of flowers, a garland or ring of flowers or a round pomander. The style and shape will largely be influenced by the overall style of the wedding and the choice of flowers. The classic choice of white and green for the bride is often accompanied by bringing out the colour of the bridesmaids' dresses in the bouquets for the attendants.

Usually bridesmaids' bouquets are not wired but loosely tied. This is the most economical choice, but if you desire a ring or a garland then your floral designer will have to wire the flowers and this will make the item more expensive. This is because more plant material and flower heads are cut up and also because of the time taken to make a wired accessory. Any wired work has to be done at the last minute, especially in a hot or humid climate.

Opposite, clockwise from top left A posy of chocolate cosmos with a long natural handle. This unusual seasonal summer flower is chocolate coloured and also smells divinely of cocoa.

A gorgeous scented hoop of mixed fragrant English sweet peas and trailing pea vines.

The cottage garden plants *Scabiosa stellata* and *S. altropurpurea* come in pink, red, white, lilac and burgundy. Known also as the pincushion flower because of its markings, scabious are often sold as a wild-flower species in seed packets.

A posy of gorgeous seasonal garden roses (these can be picked from June to September) arranged with viburnum and ivy berries is complemented by a wired headdress of rose heads and ivy.

Above A beautiful summer posy of blue and white flowers picks up the colour of the bridesmaid's dress. The blue cornflower *Centaurea cyanus* and *Scabiosa caucasica* 'Stäfa' are mixed with *Astrantia major* 'White Star', Snowflake spray roses and *Nigella damascena*.

Headdresses and hats

THE NOSTALGIC AND RETRO TREND we are currently experiencing for weddings means that hair flowers are back. Over the years they come in and out of fashion, but I think they always suit younger bridesmaids. Older bridesmaids often look better with hair flowers individually wired and professionally placed by a hair stylist. The main options are rings that sit on the crown of the head and Alice bands. Give your floral designer a head measurement to work to, although mostly they are adjustable. Your floral designer will fit them for you or instruct your hair stylist.

Above This fragrant bridesmaid head decoration is created from individually wired heads of blue hyacinth and yellow mimosa sprays. The accompanying posy has the same flowers with the addition of *Viburnum opulus*, catkins and yellow clonal ranunculus.

Opposite, clockwise from top left The other accessory that either bridesmaids, maids of honour or guests can add flowers to is hats. Individual fresh flowers look great attached to hats, as do rings around brims of larger hats. These country bridesmaids are wearing rings around their straw hats.

Bridesmaids also often wear flowers in their hair, and wired circlets and Alice bands are both very pretty. This circlet is of rosebuds with small Santini daisy chrysanthemums.

Dianthus Giant Gipsy and asters were wired with wheat to encircle the brim of these bridesmaids' hats.

Small individual rosebuds have been wired and inserted directly into the hair.

Wired circlet

A decorated band of flowers can either sit straight on the head or further back on the crown. It is very adaptable and can work with many different hairstyles, long or short, loose or formal. The band should be fitted to the head it will adorn so that it is comfortable and secure.

INGREDIENTS

25 pips of stephanotis

20 pink ranunculus

a bunch of rosemary

3 stems of green *Helleborus viridis*

10 stems of Harrington lime-green double *Helleborus hybridus*

3 stems of pink Gracia spray roses

a selection of 0.28mm (29 gauge) and 0.32mm (28 gauge) silver wires

longer green 0.72mm (21 gauge) stub wires

a roll of gutta percha tape

1 Individually wire all the flower heads with a silver wire by placing it through the calyx and then double leg-mounting by winding one wire three times over the other (see page 192 steps 2 to 3). Place two stub wires together with a silver wire to the length of the circlet you require. Cover the hoop with gutta percha tape. At each end of the wire make a hook and a loop so you can adjust the size when you fit the circlet to your bridesmaid. (You can see how the loop and hook fit together on the headdress on page 174.)

2 Taking different pieces of plant material begin to work your way along the hoop, binding the material with gutta percha and cutting off any additional wires as you go. Keeping the wires to a minimum will help to keep it light. Continue until the hoop is covered.

Opposite The bouquet has the same selection of flowers as the headdress with the addition of some Pink Piano roses. This has a deep cup shape and opens into a swirly rosette form. It is grown commercially in Colombia along with a number of other nostalgic garden roses, which are particularly popular for weddings.

Baskets and carried items

TRADITIONALLY, SMALL BRIDESMAIDS carried delicate baskets of flowers, which allowed them to put them down without damaging the flowers. Posies and pomanders can suffer at the hands of small bridesmaids and really anyone under the age of four is going to need to be supervised. Small bags, pails, pots, boxes or watering cans can make alternative containers. Rings or garlands for a group of small people can look very sweet, and teddy bears either made from moss or decorated with flowers usually score well with tiny attendants. Bracelets or wrist corsages can also work with toddlers. Younger bridesmaids and attendants often struggle with holding or wearing flowers for any length of time and so a simple wrist corsage or a small rosebud to wear is often the best way to go.

Left Frankie, a well-trained and alert Jack Russell, is entrusted as the ring bearer for a country wedding. Viburnum berries and freesias were chosen to match the markings on his fur. It is over ten years since I published my first book on wedding flowers, decorating my much-loved labrador with a floral collar. Since then we have made masses of decorations for dogs.

Opposite top A pastel watering can has been filled with spring flowers, including arching solomon's seal, magnolia buds, lilac, 'Antique' carnations, eryngium, rosebuds and *Viburnum opulus*.

Opposite below left A bracelet of gypsophila, acorns, berries and hydrangea with a ribbon tie.

Opposite below right A vintage bridesmaid's basket filled with a summery selection of cotinus, nigella seed heads, scabious, dahlias, Red Piano garden roses and *Leucanthemum* daisies.

Following spread, left A bridesmaid hands out favours at a country wedding. The table centres were gathered up into metal drinks carriers and offered to female guests to take home.

Following spread, right Turquoise is a difficult colour for flowers and so we contrasted this sequinned bridesmaid's dress with some acid-coloured dahlias and white Germini gerberas. The black seed heads are agapanthus.

Bound heart

Bunches of gypsophila have been bound to a white alice band and around a white wicker heart frame for this bridesmaid to carry.

INGREDIENTS

10 stems of Fun Time gypsophila

a length of white ribbon

small white wicker heart

a roll of 0.20mm (32 gauge) silver wire

1 Tie the ribbon to the heart. Cut small sprigs of gypsophila so that you have enough to bind round the heart.

2 Start at the top and cover over the binding wire with the next bunch. Small neat bunches added frequently will be neatest. Stop when you get to the bottom of the heart. The way to get the best shape is start again binding from the top until you meet at the bottom, and then add more sprigs of gypsophila to cover the wires at the base.

Opposite Gypsophila is great when used en masse; it looks very pretty. Choose a large flower head for this kind of design. There is also a very pretty pink gypsophila called Pinkolina, which would work well in this type of design.

BUTTONHOLES AND CORSAGES are traditionally given to immediate family and friends involved with the wedding ceremony. Many years ago it was quite common to give everyone attending a buttonhole – we did do that for one wedding last year and I have to say that we had a very positive response. We had an assortment of flowers and colours so the guests were involved in the selection process. Modern weddings have so many other gifts for guests, such as favours and goody-bags to help keep children amused, that this tradition is now largely confined to a small group.

A buttonhole is a usually a single flower with some berries and leaves. A corsage is larger and usually contains multiple heads, but it can be a single flower if it is large-headed, such as a cymbidium orchid. By far the most common choice is the rose, in a neutral colour such as white or cream to work with what the bridal party is wearing.

Buttonholes and Corsages

A peach 'Pearl Avalanche' rose buttonhole with acorns, cotoneaster berries and the grey leaves of *Brachyglottis* 'Sunshine'.

This basket shows a selection of late summer flowers that can be used for buttonholes. Miniature sunflowers and smaller dahlias are about the upper limit in terms of size.

Blue hydrangea with viburnum berries
and sprigs of rosemary and ivy.

Two Yellow Dot rosebuds with hypericum berries,
bear grass and salal leaves.

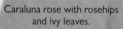

Caraluna rose with rosehips
and ivy leaves.

Scabiosa caucasica 'Clive Greaves'
with *Senecio cineraria* or dusty miller.

White phalaenopsis 'Bangalore'
with fountain grass.

'Naranga' rose with rosehip
and ruscus leaves.

A cluster bloom from *Narcissus* 'Erlicheer'
and forget-me-not with ivy leaves.

Peach Carpe Diem+ rose with rose hips
and ruscus leaves.

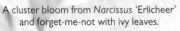

Wiring a buttonhole

If you are new to wiring, trying your hand at buttonholes is the best way to get started and perfect your technique before you attempt larger wired bouquets and arrangements.

INGREDIENTS

1 Avalanche+ rose

5 oak leaves

2 stems of acorns

0.90mm (19 gauge) and 0.71mm (21 gauge) stub wires

a selection of 0.71mm (21 gauge), 0.56mm (23 gauge) and 0.32mm (28 gauge) silver wires

a roll of gutta percha tape

pearl-headed pin

1 With wiring work it is essential to have an assortment of wires in different finishes and lengths, and generally the right wire will be just strong enough to hold the flower but not so strong that it looks rigid. I can give guidelines to the size and length you need, but it will of course depend on the size and quality of your flowers. Professional florists become adept at dealing with whatever wire they have in stock, and with practice you will too.

2 A rose of medium size will require a 0.71mm stub wire, which needs to be placed into the central stem of the rose and pushed just past the seed box. Then push a 0.56mm silver wire though the stem horizontally under the seed box.

3 Bring both wires down to the direction of the central stub wire and then twist one silver wire around the other three times. This makes sure that the head is supported and does not fall off the central wire.

4 Next wire up each leaf. Take a 0.32mm wire and stitch through the back of the main vein halfway up the leaf. Being careful not to tear the leaf, bring both ends of the silver wire down to the direction of the stems, and then twist one around the other three times.

5 Next wire up the acorns by looping a 0.56mm wire across the top of the stem and then placing one wire over the other three times to secure.

6 Next you need to tape the wired rose with the gutta percha tape. This hides the wire and makes it look more natural.

7 Tape the wire stems of all the components with gutta percha.

8 Place the five leaves around the rose head with the acorns and then tape them all into place.

9 The finished buttonhole should have a pearl-headed pin to secure it to clothing.

1

2

3

4

5

6

7

8

9

Calla lily with *Panicum* 'Fountain' grass and ruscus (left)
and peony with *Brachyglottis* 'Sunshine' (right).

Pale pink sweet pea with green berries and *Astrantia major* 'Penny's Pink' (left)
and a 'Karma Lagoon' dahlia with *Brachyglottis* 'Sunshine' leaves and Misty Bubbles rosebuds (right).

Finding the right shade of white

YOU CAN ADD A TOUCH OF ORIGINALITY AND SEASONALITY to any buttonhole by adding a sprig of greenery, berries or an additional flower. Here are some of the most readily available commercially grown white roses in varying sizes and shades. Bridal gowns are available in so many shades of white, cream and ivory that it can be really difficult to decide which is the best white rose to work with your dress.

Below Wonderfully fragrant and petally, Norma Jeane is a large-headed rose used here with a sprig of white heather and dark ivy leaves. Patience, Alabaster, Vitality or White O'Hara are also wonderfully natural and fragrant.

Below A rosebud from an Avalanche+ spray rose has been wired with holly leaves and a moss rose. This is a mutation of a rose, where the calyx and sepal create a mossy ball. You can find these on wild dog roses or purchase hybrid Moss roses – these were first popular with the Victorians who relished such natural curiosities.

Below White Magic is a hybrid tea rose. Wired here with snowberries and olive leaves, it makes a perfect autumn combination. Blanchette is also a lovely rounded spray rose with a hint of pink in the centre. If you are searching for something peachier, try Jana spray roses.

Above The spray rose 4 Good White+ is appropriately named for a wedding. This little bud is great for small buttonholes, wired here with brown hypericum and green rosehips. Snowflake is a good alternative. For a creamier rose bud look at Cream Garcia or Cream Sensation.

Above White O'Hara is a beautiful bridal white rose, shown here with fern and jade hypericum. This is a bud from a Dutch commercially grown spray rose, which is a hydrid of the garden rose. You can also buy commercially grown garden roses. White Lydia would be a good alternative for a neat small bud.

There are no truly pure white roses, with the closest to white being Akito. For an old-fashioned scented rose, you may plump for Norma Jeane or the David Austin garden rose Patience. For a good-shaped rose, I often like to use Avalanche+ or White Naomi. The warmer almost peach tone of Vendela is also the most popular choice for ivory gowns.

Below Dolomiti is an absolutely stunning creamy-white medium-headed rose with a high petal count, wired here with stephanandra and white astrantia. If you like the shape but want your rose to be a touch creamier, consider Artemis.

Below Avalanche+ is the queen of white roses with its large head, high petal count and sturdy strength. This white rose, with a hint of green around the outer petals, has been the most popular wedding rose as it opens fully to resemble a garden rose but holds its petals for much longer. Avalanche+ took over from Tineke roses in Europe, but some are still grown in South America.

Above Akito is the purest white rose. It has a medium-sized head so is popular for buttonholes or tight bouquets. Escimo, Athena, Polo, Tibet and Bianca are similar medium-sized white roses, but are more open and less pure in colour. Here Akito is wired with a wild thistle and an eryngium head and edged with ivy leaves – perfect for a Scottish-themed wedding.

Above Vendela and Talea are creamy roses with tight heads that make great buttonholes, rose posies and pomanders. Trimmed here with viburnum berries and cotinus leaves for an autumnal feel, this is a champagne ivory rose and one of our most popular for ivory wedding gowns. Renate is slightly deeper and peachier.

The Ceremony

TRADITIONALLY, THE LOCATION for the wedding ceremony was determined by religious affiliation, personal family or convenience to family and friends. Nowadays, these considerations rarely figure – in fact, many brides and grooms go out of their way to make their wedding a destination event. More relaxed licensing laws on wedding ceremonies mean that more destinations have been released for ceremonies, widening the choice of venue. Outdoor weddings are allowed and popular in some countries and cultures. Whatever the choice of venue, there is usually some floral decoration at the focus of the wedding vows.

Increasingly popular in recent times is to have a venue that allows you to have your ceremony and your reception in the same place. This keeps the party together and allows for a better flow of events during the day. Currently, historic houses and castles are very popular to host both events. Many hotels also offer you the chance to hold your ceremony and reception in the same space.

Left A succulent, guelder rose and Germini gerbera detail from a mandap decoration for a Hindu ceremony (see pages 159 and 200 top).

Opposite A Catholic church is decorated with two pedestals of flowers featuring Yvonne, Peach Delight and Nuit d'Été' dahlias to frame the bride and groom, pew ends down the nave of the church and a floral garland across the gallery.

Church weddings

THE FOCUS FOR A CHURCH WEDDING is always the central aisle, and that is why it is customary to line it with pew ends and frame the area where the bride and groom will make their vows with two pedestals of flowers. Each church has other unique features that you might want to decorate with flowers. Sometimes it can be a pulpit or a font, or often it will be an arch around the door where some formal wedding photographs can be taken of the processional and the recessional.

Scale is an important consideration – it is much harder to make some impact in a vast cathedral than in a small village church. Your floral designer will advise you on the best places to display your flowers, and it is always important to check with the authorities at the church what decorations you are permitted to have. Some churches have flower-arranging teams that can help with the flowers. These are largely amateurs, however, and the standards can be alarmingly unpredictable!

Above and opposite top The church featured two pulpits and so we decided to decorate both to add to the symmetry. The glass vase was positioned near the signing of the register following the vows.

Below and opposite bottom An outdoor chuppah is decorated with hanging amaranthus, artichoke flowers, roses and lilies. The detail of the base of the chuppah pole shows how the plant material – artichoke flowers, dianthus, lilies, ornamental kales and berries – is arranged in a natural and holistic way.

Outdoor weddings

OUTDOOR WEDDINGS ARE ENJOYED in most countries, such as the United States and Australia, but are not yet legal in England and Wales, although they are permitted in Scotland. Discussions are underway to make outdoor wedding ceremonies legal in all of the UK, but at present you can only be married outdoors at a licensed venue and by an authorized religious or civil official, and you have to sign the register indoors under a roof with a fixed address. However, if you are having a Jewish ceremony you can get married anywhere you like as long as you are under a chuppah, or wedding canopy. You can hire a chuppah or it can be made for you, usually by your floral designers or the production team on your wedding. I have had the pleasure of decorating many outdoor chuppahs. One on the banks of the River Thames and another on the lawns of Highclere Castle (made famous as the location for the television series *Downton Abbey*) stick in my mind as wonderful venues on gloriously sunny days.

Multi-faith ceremonies

MANDAPS ARE CANOPIES similar to chuppahs, but the wedding party is seated for part of the ceremony, whereas at a Jewish ceremony the wedding parties stand under the chuppah. A Hindu priest officiates at the ceremony and numerous relatives perform specific roles under his guidance. Hindu weddings vary according to the historic culture of the family. Muslim weddings also vary enormously depending on the culture and where the family originated. Muslims come from very different cultures and so a Turkish Muslim wedding will be very different from a Pakistani or African wedding. For most Muslims it is the Islamic ceremony that counts and not the confirmation in the registry office. In the UK, for example, the majority of mosques have not been officially registered for weddings, and so this often means Muslims marrying in the UK will have two ceremonies, one religious and one legal.

Above and opposite top A mandap is viewed through decorations hanging from the trees. The frame has been decorated with *Tillandsia xerographica*, 'Kermit' Germini gerberas, 'Pole Ice' gerberas and *Virburnum opulus*. A gypsophila and cymbidium orchid runner lines the aisle. Although these flowers might seem like unlikely bedfellows, they both last well out of water and so are perfect for this detail.

Below and opposite bottom This rustic licensed venue has been simply decorated with one central arrangement of French tulips and magnolia branches and lots of ivy and pillar candles. Metal pots of planted hellebores line the aisles.

Licensed venues for civil ceremonies

MANY STATELY HOMES, civic buildings, hotels and public buildings are awarded a licence to hold marriages and civil partnerships. This has widened the choice of venue for couples and has led to more individual and original weddings that are very relaxed in nature as everything happens in one venue. However, be aware that some venues exercise control over the suppliers you might use, including florists, putting together a suggested list of vendors. Some venues require a percentage fee from all their recommended suppliers, and so this can add to the costs or compromise what is being supplied. It also compromises your freedom to use the suppliers you would like.

Decorating columns

INGREDIENTS

10 bunches of ivy trails
Hedera helix

8 bunches of trails of
Clematis vitalba

4 bunches of trailing
asparagus fern

100 heritage dahlias (we
used 'Peach Delight',
'Yvonne', 'Nuit d´Éte',
'Anna Lindh', 'Wittemans
Best', 'Gay Princess',
'Apricot Desire' and
'Ludwig Helfert')

60 old-fashioned bloom
chrysanthemums

10 bunches of wild dog
rose hips

30 *Panicum* 'Fountain'

8 floral foam Florettes

strong cable ties

2.5-cm (1-inch) chicken
wire

1 First you need to secure the soaked floral foam Florettes around the column evenly. We secured a cable tie at the top and also around the base for extra security, and then covered them with chicken wire.

2 When you are happy that the ties are really tight and the mechanics are safe and evenly spaced to avoid gaps in the final display you can begin to arrange the plant material. You need different types of foliage. We started with the downward trails of ivies. Build up the foliage between the floral foam so that the greenery appears as a circle around the top rather than as separate arrangements. We always get the shape we want before we add any flowers.

3 Start to add the flowers, mixing up the colours as much as possible. Dahlias and chrysanthemums can shatter if knocked, so you have to take your time with these flowers. Add the arching wild hips.

4 Add the fountain grass to fill any gaps at the end to finish the arrangement.

Many grand venues have columns that lend themselves to decoration. With permission it is amazing what you can achieve with a bag of cable ties! It helps if there are some ridges or decoration that you can use, but generally cable ties or zip-wires hold a fair amount of weight very firmly. Originally used by electricians, you can buy cable ties in many strengths and sizes. A basic toolbox is essential for this type of in situ decorating and most likely a ladder.

Left and below The decorated columns make a great floral frame for wedding party photographs. The central arrangement is of roses, lilies, chrysanthemums, dahlias, hanging amaranthus, asparagus fern and contorted willow.

Floral arch

Arches are a great way to frame the wedding ceremony and one of my own personal favourites to construct. Arches can be made on metal frames or you can make up your own frame from birch and willow so it fits the doorway exactly. We do a mixture of both; the advantage of this method is that it is freestanding rather than attached to the building.

INGREDIENTS

10 bunches of contorted willow

20 bunches of *Eucalyptus pulverulenta* 'Baby Blue'

10 bunches of rosemary

10 bunches of 'Amazing Fantasy' rose hips

10 bunches of *Symphoricarpos* Charming Fantasy

50 *Hydrangea macrophylla* 'Alpenglühen'

50 *Hydrangea macrophylla* 'Sibilla'

60 Purple Power roses

60 Karma Sangria dahlias

60 Purple Flame dahlias

60 Misty Bubbles spray roses

100 Maritim roses

60 Ruby Red roses

60 *Viburnum opulus*

100 stems of poppy seed heads

10 bunches of *Brachyglottis* 'Sunshine'

60 stems of red trailing amaranthus

birch poles cemented into two sturdy pots (see page 99 step 2)

a roll of heavy bind wire

16 floral foam blocks

2.5-cm (1-inch) chicken wire to run the length of the frame

Opposite Pink, purple and lime green has always been a treasured colour combination of mine, and is still my favourite.

1 Place birch poles the height of the door frame either side of the door and cover with twisted willow. Wire together the willow to create the arch, attaching it to the top of each pole. Next wrap the floral foam blocks in chicken wire and start to attach to the arch.

2 Continue adding the floral foam. Cover with more chicken wire and continue to work on the mechanics until you are sure the arch is stable and will not move.

3 Start by using foliage to fill out the whole frame. It is important to take a look from afar occasionally to make sure the shape is looking good.

4 Begin adding the most dominant flowers, such as the hydrangeas, and then add smaller flowers in groups to make more impact. Finally, place the trailing amaranthus so that it looks as though the whole thing has been growing there all the time.

Large-scale pedestal

I vary my mechanics for large arrangements depending on what plant material I am using and how long the design needs to last. In spring and summer we have long and plentiful plant material so I often arrange in water so all the soft plant material can drink freely. If the arrangement is more structured and precise I use foam, and if the plant material is shorter I would choose foam or 5-cm (2-inch) chicken wire to give the flowers height.

INGREDIENTS

10 stems of magnolia branches

5 stems of long olive branches

15 stems of *Prunus cerasifera* 'Nigra'

110 each of 'Maiden's Blush' and 'Hugo Koster' lilac

10 *Viburnum opulus* 'Roseum'

10 each of 'Blue Skies' and Candle Lavender Group delphiniums

20 *Matthiola incana* 'Figora Light Rose' (stocks)

10 stems of ivy trails *Hedera helix*

10 stems of *Polygonatum multiflorum* (Solomon's seal)

20 Cool Water roses

10 'Robina' lilies

plastic bucket set in a large urn with moss

1 Secure the bucket into the container with moss so the edge is proud of the urn. Add water mixed with flower food.

2 Next establish a frame for the flowers using branches of magnolia.

3 When you have a good structure you can begin to add the foliage. You should aim to make the arrangement at least one and a half times as high as the urn to create a visually pleasing effect.

4 Next add the longer stems and the fuller flowers of the lilac and viburnum.

5 Add the tall spires of delphinium and stocks throughout the arrangement. Use the ivy and Solomon's seal to trail over the edge of the urn – this creates a natural feel.

6 Finally add the roses and the lilies in any gaps to create a massed flower effect.

The
Reception

ON YOUR WEDDING DAY the reception is always going to be the part of the proceedings that takes most of the day, and so this is where most people want to allocate more of their floral budget. Along with the flowers, there are lots of other associated style considerations, such as the table linen, the types of chairs, lighting and accessories. Your floral designer will help you make the most of the reception venue, working within your budget constraints. The main consideration is how many guests you are inviting, as each table will require some form of decoration and this is usually the largest chunk of the budget.

Right One large urn on a plinth makes a focal point for an entrance. This early summer combination includes 'Gladiator' alliums, wild lilac, 'Corso' lilies, guelder roses, *Fritillaria persica*, 'Sarah Bernhardt' peonies and branches of *Sorbus aria* 'Lutescens' and eucalyptus.

Opposite Inexpensive baskets or handmade containers are perfect for table flowers, as the guests can take the table centres home and enjoy the decorations for longer.

208

All floral designers will recommend having one or two spectacular displays, but bridal couples usually want decorations all over the place so there is often a compromise on what will work best. One way of making a striking impact is to use monochromatic colours or all one type of flower. This is visually more arresting and makes a lot of impact. If you can agree on something colourful and seasonal, this is the most economical way to go.

When you look at a venue space without guests, you often focus on lots of areas where flowers may not turn out to be necessary, as they will be hidden from view among all your guests. It is always a good idea to visit your reception venue just before someone else's wedding so you can get a better feel for it. Flowers on plinths or raised up on mantels over fireplaces make more impact than lots of small displays.

If you have a lot of space to decorate it is more economical to use trees or large architectural plants alongside more elaborate floral constructions. Sometimes it is possible to hire these, so making the decorations less costly and extravagant.

Opposite These grand candelabras were designed for an autumnal wedding with a Dutch Old Masters theme. The bride and groom had already decided on the rich colours of purple and orange when I first met with them, and this is the outcome of our design meetings.

Above right Heavy metal candelabras have been completely hidden under a mass of green ivies and stems of physalis, or Chinese lanterns. The top of the candelabras has been filled with carthamus, ornamental kales, kniphofia, hanging green amaranthus, arbutus berries, *Cynara cardunculus*, Fair Jewel and Magic Pearl rosehips, *Calendula officinalis* 'Green Spot Orange' and 'Cartouche-Shakyra' dahlias.

Below right Fabric draped from a central chandelier has been garlanded around the top of the four columns with dahlias, arbutus berries, ornamental kales, physalis and green hanging amaranthus.

Table settings

Below left We were able to suspend glass votives filled with delicate small-headed 'Venice' mini phalaenopsis orchids above this sophisticated lime-green table setting.

THE TABLE DECORATION IS GOING to be determined largely by the table shape. Round banqueting tables are the most common, but in recent years there has been a trend to have rectangular tables, which are easier to talk across. Other considerations are the ceiling height of the room and how much decoration it requires. Ballrooms with thirty tables often look best with a selection of flower arrangements in varying heights. While one does not want the flowers to cause an obstruction in the middle of the table, it is in any case very difficult to make yourself heard across a large table, and so it makes more sense to have some elevated flower designs in the centre of a number of the tables.

Above We wanted to add a little more colour to this room and so we used lime green fabric over the top of the chair backs and trimmed each one with a large phalaenopsis 'Kobe' – one of my favourite large-headed varieties for weddings.

Opposite Down the centre is a very textural combination of flowers and foliages in muted silvers and whites, but with a little of the acid green. The air plants are *Tillandsia xerographica* and the base of foliage is *Brachyglottis* 'Sunshine' and *Alchemilla mollis*. The rose is the very square-edged and petally Dolomiti. The white gerbera is 'Pole Ice', one of the purest white gerberas, and the green mini gerbera is 'Kermit'. There are also a few stems of the 'Venice' phalaenopsis woven through the design to tie the hanging decoration to the table.

Linear table centre

Long tables look smart with full, low flower arrangements, and they are more conducive to conversation than wider circular tables. Beware though that some banqueting tables can be as narrow as 90cm (3 feet) and this does not really allow for any great width in the decorations as sufficient space needs to be allowed for table settings otherwise the overall effect will be very cluttered.

INGREDIENTS

3 bunches of camellia foliage

5 bunches of flowering photinia

3 bunches of seasonal purple tree lilac

10 stems of 'Maiden's Blush' lilac

40 Peach Avalanche+ roses

30 cream clonal ranunculus

30 *Viburnum opulus*

20 'Coral Charm' peonies

20 'Duchesse de Nemours' peonies

50 fringed 'Huis ten Bosch' tulips

1-m (39-inch) floral foam Raquette

1

2

3

4

5

6

1 Soak the foam for ten minutes until the bubbles cease to rise in the water. Taking the camellia foliage in lengths of around 12cm (5 inches), work your way across the centre of the foam so that it is placed in all directions from the centre line.

2 Work down to the table edge and up to a height of around 10cm (4 inches) so that the foliage covers the whole block with no foam showing. Taking the flowery sprigs of the photinia work across from end to end.

3 Then take the lilacs and, raising them slightly higher than the foliage, give the arrangement some life with these dancing blossoms.

4 Next add the roses, zig-zagging across the centre of the design and down to the table edge.

5 The ranunculus will need careful handling, so grip them close to the foam when you push the stem of these flowers into the foam. Spread the colour across the oasis frame.

6 Add the lime-green viburnum into any dark gaps and to trail over the edge of the foam and onto the table. Add the peonies into good focal spots so they can be enjoyed. Then take the tulips and carefully place their stems into any gaps, using the length of their stems to lighten the ends and sides.

This gorgeous spring table arrangement is set on
a tablecloth to match the wallpaper at the elegant
Jockey Club in Newmarket.

Left Chatting through candlelight is the most romantic thing to do. My gorgeous clients for this wedding wanted to use candelabras in a modern way, and as one of them had Scandinavian roots I decided to use these Swedish candelabras and colourful Danish candles.

Left They both wanted really colourful displays and so we decided to reflect the candles in the flowers and use different colours on each table. The purple arrangements are decorated with lilac, *Viburnum opulus*, 'Blue Diamond' tulips, 'Pauline' tulips and 'Woodstock' hyacinths. The pink variations use 'Super Green' Parrot tulips, Acqua! roses and pink ranunculus with *Viburnum opulus* and mossed twigs.

Above On the day, each flower designer had the opportunity to work on her own design, rather than making twenty arrangements that looked identical. Some of the best parties and weddings I have designed have not had matching arrangements, and blocking colour like this is very striking. The orange-red candles were complemented by 'Orange Juice' ranunculus and 'Orange Monarch' tulips.

The eclectic versus the simple. A collection of vases is a very interesting way to decorate a table (opposite), particularly a long table, but this bohemian look is not cheap to put together. The florist needs lots of hardware to choose from and also an interesting combination of flowers to make the look coordinate. As it is more visual and less controlled it requires a bigger range and budget.

The simplicity of the snake's head fritillaria plants in this plastic pot covered with moss (right) is a complete contrast but still arresting. The cost is a fraction of the table scape on the left, but it is as beautiful and as unusual. Think about plants if your budget is limited, as you really can get an extraordinary effect for a very reasonable price. Bulbs in winter work well, summer has endless possibilities and in autumn you could think about a collection of interesting gourds or members of the squash family.

Opposite Copper heart-shaped vases are filled with artichoke flowers, pink snowberries, ornamental kales, red hanging amaranthus, guelder rose, rosemary, stocks campanula, dahlias and hydrangea.

Right The cut-flower season for fritillaria is very short, but if planted the flowers are available a little longer. They make a very dainty table centre.

Clockwise from top left A rolled white linen napkin tied with grosgrain ribbon and a small posy of scabious with dusty miller foliage.

A fanned napkin trimmed with a cream bow and a single dahlia with some arbutus berries.

Physalis and thlaspi decorate a flat, folded white napkin.

A more intricately folded napkin calls for simpler decoration, in this case a striking combination of the *Echinacea* 'Green Jewel' with a small red apple.

Below A single large artichoke flower of *Cynara cardunculus* Scolymus Group. This species of thistle, cultivated for food, produces a very handsome flower.

Opposite A wedding lunch with a Provence theme uses lavender for the votives, and sunflowers, hydrangea and achillea in the main display. Ivy and arbutus foliage make the base, with Yellow Dot spray roses dotted through. Small bunches, trimmed with blue ribbon, also adorn the napkins.

Floral napkins

THIS HAS TO BE THE SIMPLEST and the easiest way to get involved with decorating your table. Your caterers will source the napkins for you and all you have to do is add a flower or a seed head. If you are good with ribbon, there are endless opportunities.

Personally, I like napkins to be flat or rolled, but I admit the more elaborate folded designs can all look lovely in the right environment and with the correct flowers. There are whole books on napkin folding and a wealth of choices. Don't fall out with your partner stressing about all these minute details! If you are in doubt, take the advice of your caterer and floral designer and know they will guide you well from their own experience.

Chair backs

ADDING DECORATIONS to the backs of the chairs can transform your reception venue. The decoration can be rustic, such as a hessian bow or a willow heart, or just be a single flower tied in place. At many of the weddings we decorate, the chair backs from the ceremony are repositioned in the reception area so they can continue to be enjoyed. Depending on how many there are, these usually end up on the top table. You could reserve the chair backs just for the bride and groom, to mark out their place in the room. Once or twice I have decorated every chair in a reception, but it has normally been with a single flower such as a calla lily or a rose.

Above left Campanula, ornamental kale, cotinus (or smokebush), a Barbie rose and rosemary form the linear decoration on the back of a pretty white-painted wooden chair.

Left Continuing the colour theme, the bridesmaid carries a posy of scabious and has a few heads wired into her ponytail.

Opposite, above A loose chair back for the bridegroom is made from mixed foliages with astilbe, gloriosa, Carpe Diem+ roses and rosehips. The heart for the bride's seat is bound with hydrangea, gypsophila, rosehips and Catalina, Pearl Avalanche+ and Carpe Diem+ roses.

Opposite, below left Avalanche+ roses and Sweet Avalanche+ spray roses, with some *Ammi visnaga* heads, are tucked into a generous silk bow on the back of a fabric-covered chair.

Opposite, below right Individual 'Largo' double tulip and Black Baccara rose heads have been threaded onto wire to create these striking linear chair garlands.

Left A pink glass bowl filled with roses, peonies, celosia, asclepias, 'Annabelle' hydrangea, carthamus, kniphofia and bright pink and orange roses is positioned in a side area.

Below Filled with blue hydrangea, a glass fishbowl is topped with a hand-tied bouquet of Vendela roses, lysimachia, cornflowers, dill, white veronica, *Ammi majus* and *Daucus carota* 'Dara', with a touch of white snowberries and *Anethum graveolens*. Loose hydrangea heads are also strewn among the place names.

Side tables

APART FROM THE MAIN DINING TABLES there are often other key areas at a wedding reception venue where guests will gather that can be adorned with an arrangement of flowers. One such place is the coat-check room. Another area to which guests will be sure to turn their attention is the seating plan or place card table, so placing a bowl of flowers or two here will elicit plenty of interest and appreciation. You can even consider having a chill-out area or a relaxation zone, designed for use later in the evening. Sometimes this is an opportunity to use a different style of flowers than you have gone with for the rest of the day.

Opposite A chill-out area at Gaynes Park in Essex was given a Moroccan theme. Tall glass vases filled with *Gloriosa superba* 'Rothschildiana' are set on a bed of Naomi roses. Strelitzia, commonly known as bird of paradise, can be seen in the larger display vases poking into the photograph on the left.

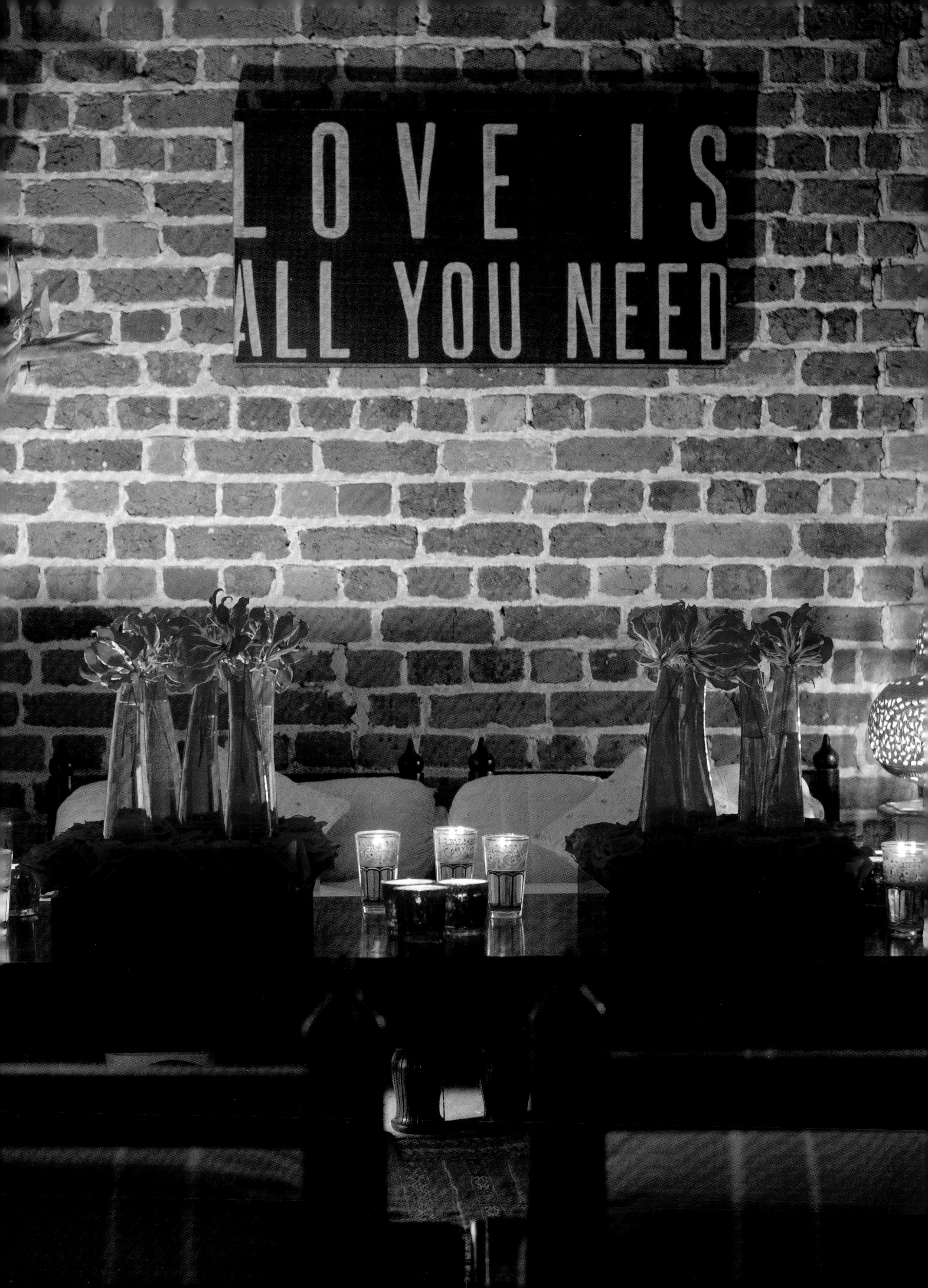
LOVE IS
ALL YOU NEED

Hot pepper arrangement

Fruit and vegetables have featured in my work often. The inspiration can come from art from looking at Dutch Masters or just from an early morning foray over to the Covent Garden vegetable market in London. Whenever I go abroad to demonstrate, you will always find me at a local market the day before looking for some edible inspiration.

INGREDIENTS

a catering box of orange capsicum peppers

25 smaller chiquino peppers

a bunch of fruiting ivy

urn

2 blocks of dried floral foam

a bundle of 30-cm (12-inch) bamboo skewers

1 Secure the foam into the urn upright so that it makes a tall shape.

2 Push the skewers into the peppers, but without coming right through, then add them to the base of the arrangement around the lip of the urn.

3 Where you have gaps and see the foam, place a sprig of ivy. Continue building up the peppers in rings until you reach the top.

Above and opposite Urns are a classic shape and work so well with flowers and fruit. These iron ones I have used on so many occasions and with hundreds of different paint finishes. At the moment I am enjoying working with some neon colours. Over the years, the inspired caterers we have worked for have asked us to make designs to decorate their food stations. The peppers were used for a Mexican food station and the strawberries adorned a scrummy dessert station.

Strawberry tree

Food bars are always a key gathering point at weddings and a great place to exhibit an interesting flower design.

INGREDIENTS

a bunch of birch twigs

a large grapefruit (or pomelo)

8 punnets of strawberries

20 dahlias

cement

a small pole or stick

a terracotta pot

a roll of reel wire

a bag of knotted bamboo picks

a red cube vase

sand

a block of green floral foam

1 First cement the pole into the centre of the terracotta pot and leave to set. When the cement is hard, use reel wire to bind some birch twigs around the central pole to give it an interesting texture and to make it look natural.

2 Impale the grapefruit securely onto the top of the pole. Place a knotted bamboo pick through the green top of a strawberry and secure into the grapefruit.

3 To create a good-sized strawberry head you need to leave a gap between the grapefruit and the strawberries. The head of your strawberry tree needs to be about the same size as the base to look in proportion.

4 Place the pot in the vase. Fill with sand to add some ballast and make the pot secure. Now add a little green floral foam to the top of the vase so that you can add a collar of dahlia heads.

Cakes

The wedding cake is the focal point of the reception. Traditionally it was a fruit cake, but more often, couples now choose different flavours for different tiers. There are lots of alternative ideas, such as croquembouche, macaroons, cupcakes, mini-desserts or even a tower of cheeses. Your floral designer and your cake provider will often liaise over the table decoration and flowers. We often do a ring of flowers or a garland to decorate the cake.

Cake ring and topper

You don't want your cake and your flowers fighting for centre stage. With this gorgeous cake designed by Cakes by Krishanthi, we chose to do a ring at the base and a small cake topper. For this cake we have dampened the foam so the flowers can drink and stay fresh. Even in countries where having a wedding cake was previously not the custom, cakes are becoming very popular through blogs and social media. In the UK, it is customary to cut the cake, make a wish and have a toast of Champagne.

INGREDIENTS

30 stems of lilac

100 heads of David Austin garden roses

a bunch of jasmine

half a block of floral foam

a wreath frame that is slightly larger than your bottom tier

a plastic or polystyrene drinking cup

1 Soak the floral foam and the frame. Cut the block to fit in the cup for the topper – it needs to be twice as high as the cup. Position the cake on a cake stand in the centre of the frame. Stand back to make sure it looks central from all angles. Begin to add the flowers in the ring, placing the lilac between the roses and building round and filling the gap created by the cake stand. Weave some jasmine trails through the flowers to make it look like a vine growing in a garden.

2 For the topper, you need to cut the stems of your roses very short as you do not have a great depth of foam and you don't want to make it crumble. You can see in the photograph how you have to angle the roses into the foam so they cover the plastic container to make the roses look natural. Fill any gaps with lilac and then add jasmine trails as for the base.

The petally roses mimic the delicate ruffles of icing on the lowest tier of this beautiful peach cake.

Tiered cake

It all started with *Martha Stewart Weddings* magazine displaying gorgeous simple cakes with bands of flowers mixed in between – twenty years on, they are still featuring in many of my weddings! I think the flowers work best when the design of the cake itself is kept plain and simple.

INGREDIENTS

a selection of roses and dahlias – each tier needs between 60–100 heads depending on head size

3 tiers of cake – we used a 15-cm (6-inch), a 20-cm (8-inch) and a 25-cm (10-inch) tier

2 blocks of floral foam

some plastic film

a plastic or polystyrene drinking cup

1 These tiered cakes with flowers look better if they are thinner and leaner, and the more bands the better. Starting with the bottom tier set the cake up and add a piece of plastic film to protect the cake from the foam. The best way to approach this is to use dry foam and create the arrangement just before the wedding party are due. Or – if you are having a reveal – just before the cake is going to be presented. Build up the layers of cake and foam, cut to size, protecting each tier from foam and taking care to make your foam central so the cake still looks upright from all angles.

2 Add the flowers so that they are flush with the bigger tier of the cake. It is best to go round in sections so that it is neat and all the foam is concealed. This is a job for a patient and calm person and you need to take your time.

3 For the cake top use the cup as a small receptacle for the floral foam. Make sure that the foam is reasonably high so that you can create quite a thick tier of flowers for the top and place flowers at right angles, so the cup is concealed from view by the flowers (see step 2 page 228.).

Opposite Cutting the cake is always a photo opportunity and at this country wedding a garden gazebo makes a beautiful backdrop.

FLOWER
PALETTES

WITH THE INTERNATIONAL SUPPLY OF FLOWERS around the world, you can pretty much have whatever colour scheme you desire for your wedding at whatever time of year you choose to wed – at a price.

Locally grown seasonal flowers will always be less expensive, however, and will give your flowers a very personal and memorable feel. Each season has its own dominant palette and the beginning of the year celebrates pastels, offering us lots of small and delicate beauties. Many are so exquisite they almost demand to be viewed in isolation, and I think this is a good time to use planted arrangements of bulbs, hellebores or primroses.

HELLEBORUS X HYBRIDUS BRADFIELD SLATE

VIBURNUM TINUS

HELLEBORUS X HYBRIDUS HARRINGTON DOUBLE GREEN

PRIMULA VULGARIS

Early Spring

Everyone adores spring when, after months of dormant ground and leafless trees, the sap begins to rise and the bulbs push up through the ground. Valentine's Day is a popular day for weddings and by the time we get to mid February there is a tantalizing array of bulb and tuber production, and also some fantastic early foliage and blossoms. I love designing wedding schemes with branches of blossom, catkins, pussy willow, bulb flowers and mosses in early spring. It is a great time for using scent: many narcissus are scented, and hyacinths are also heavily fragranced. Muscari, hellebores, snowflakes, fritillaria, violets and camellia are all wonderful nostalgic flowers and currently very popular, with the trend for natural garden flowers.

Above Hellebores and fritillaria make an informal posy for a spring bride or bridesmaid.

CAMELLIA JAPONICA 'CAMPELLI' GUICHARD

HELLEBORUS X HYBRIDUS HARRINGTON SINGLE

GALANTHUS

PRUMULA VERIS

NARCISSUS 'TÊTE-À-TÊTE'

FORSTYTHIA X INTERMEDIA 'SPECTABILIS'.

HYACINTHUS ORIENTALIS 'CARNEGIE'

ACACIA BAILEYANA 'PURPUREA'.

NARCISSUS 'ICE FOLLIES'

VIBURNUM OPULUS 'ROSEUM'.

ANEMONE CORONARIA 'GALIL WIT.'

TULIPA 'DYNASTY'

SYRINGEA VULGARIS 'RUHM VON HORSTENSTEIN.'

'APRICOT BLEND' RANUNCULUS

SALIX CAPREA

TULIPA 'MAUREEN'

MAGNOLIA

Late Spring

By the time we get to the spring equinox, there is a myriad of colours to choose for your wedding scheme. Tulips come in every conceivable colour – deepest purple, vibrant primary colours and also some delicate marbled parrots and fringed pastels. The vibrant *Viburnum opulus* 'Roseum' makes any colour scheme zing and there is no better time to champion yellow, the most cheerful and sunny of colours. The wonderfully scented yellow mimosa would be a very romantic option. My favourite flowers for this season are the ranunculus, which come in an amazing array of deep and bright colours as well as pastels. Branches and blossom and early spring greens are also at their best. It is a great time for using scent, as hyacinths, mimosa and lilac are also gloriously fragrant, and this is the best time for the gorgeous scent of jasmine, too. When we approach May Day, we have the most regal of scents in season, with lily of the valley being such a popular bridal flower. Late spring also brings the first of two other ever-popular wedding scents – sweet peas and stocks.

Above The peach tulip 'Maureen' nestles among stems of *Salix caprea* 'Snow Flake'.

Summer Blues

Summer presents the happy couple and the floral designer with the widest range of flowers at their most plentiful and usually at their least expensive. Annuals grown from seed or perennials are abundant, and from late May to September there is much to be harvested locally. This is the best time to get married if you want to use indigenous flowers, or if you want to try to grow some for your own wedding. It is also in this season that plant material reaches great heights, and so it is often easier to get 1-m (3-feet) or 1.5-m (4-feet) lengths for large installations.

The summer season is the best season for blue flowers and you really can get huge variety, from pale blue through to the deepest cobalt and as near as we get to navy in the plant kingdom. There is also a great diversity in shape and scale. I adore the soft cottage garden flowers, such as love-in-a-mist and sweet pea, or varieties that can be found in the wild such as cornflowers or scabious. These make lovely flowers for posies and small table centres. The stronger and spiky echinops and eryngium can be used for a range of wedding arrangements for texture and colour. I carried eryngium in my own bridal bouquet, and I love to use sprigs attached to buttonholes. For scent use lavender or flowering mint, which are both refreshing foliages to use at this time of year. Another small almost insignificant blue flower I adore is veronica, which gives movement and structure to all kinds of summer designs.

DELPHINIUM 'IVOR ARROW'

ECHINOPS RITRO 'VEITCH'S BLUE'

DELPHINIUM 'ALIE DUYVESTEYN'

ERYNGIUM ALPINUM

SCABIOUS CAUSCASICA 'STÄFA'

AGAPANTHUS

EUSTOMA 'PICCOLO LILAC'

CENTAUREA CYANUS

HYDRANGEA MACROPHYLLA 'CHALLENGE BLUE'

Left A collar of hydrangea surrounds a vase of 'Secret' delphinium for a summer wedding.

ORIGANUM MARJORANA

CONVALLARIA MAJALIS

VERONICA 'DARK MARTJE'

NIGELLA DAMASCENA

LAVANDULA ANGUSTIFOLA 'HIDCOTE'

MISCANTHUS SINENSIS 'MALEPARTUS'

AGAPANTHUS SEED

CLEMATIS INSPIRATION

ECHINACEA PURPUREA 'FATAL ATTRACTION'

AGAPANTHUS

ECHINOPS RITRO 'VEITCH'S BLUE'

ECHINOPS RITRO 'VEITCH'S BLUE'

VIBURNUM OPULUS 'ROSEUM'

DAUCUS CAROTA 'DARA'

DIANTHUS BARBATUS 'GREEN TRICK'

SCABIOUS

LEUCANTHEMUM VULGARE 'MAIKON'

EUPATORIUM PURPUREUM

TUBEROSE

COTINUS COGGYGRIA 'ROYAL PURPLE'

DAHLIA 'TAMBURO'

CAMPANULA MEDIUM PINK

SWEET PEA

ZINNIA ELEGANS

GERATUM 'BLUE HORIZION'

CAMPANULA MEDIUM 'CHAMPION BLUE'

ORIGANUM MARJORANA

ERYNGIUM ALPINUM

NTIA MAJOR 'ROMA'

PAEONIA 'SARAH BERNHARDT'

LUPIN

VERONICA 'ANNA'

DIANTHUS GIANT GIPSY

PHLOX

ROSA GERTRUDE JEKYLL

CINDERELLA

High Summer

Plentiful and easy on the pocket – high summer is the time to get married if you like cottage-garden flowers and the wild and natural look. Each season suggests a style and the loose spires of delphinium, campanula and lupins work best in informal arrangements. If you prefer a more structured look for your summer wedding you might consider a scheme just using roses. The use of one type of flower always makes a wedding look more formal and ordered. Lilies are also very grand and elegant, and peonies, either on their own or with a touch of *Alchemilla mollis*, look stunning in any venue.

Summer is the perfect time for vintage flowers such as scented phlox, astrantia, ageratum, daisies, columbines, cosmos and pinks. There is no shortage of thistles, with cirsium, ernygiums in all shapes and also echinops. For foliages, summer is the peak time for grasses, which add a natural backdrop to flower arrangements. Excellent grasses are miscanthus, panicitum and *Briza media* (quaking grass), and wheat, oats and barley are also reaching maturity at this time of the year. Summer fragrances include roses, lilies, honeysuckle and tuberose. If you are looking for a more aromatic scent, try marigolds, chocolate cosmos, flowering nicotiana, lemon-scented geraniums or tansy. If you are planning a garden or marquee reception try evening-scented flowers in pots, such as nicotiana, evening primrose and night-scented stocks, which will make your moonlit party sensuous and sweet.

Above Pink, purple and green is one of my favoured summer colour combinations. This side table vase is full of roses, campanula, hydrangea and dahlias. The curved burgundy grasses are *Setaria italica* 'Red Jewel'.

Late Summer

The palette of late summer starts to get more fiery and textural. Vivid flowers and berries can be dramatic as this season takes on the jewel colours of the late summer border. This is a lovely time to start to take advantages of some of the berries that are beginning to form, such as blackberries, snowberries, chilli peppers and red *Viburnum opulus* berries and the blue berries of *Viburnum tinus*. Seed-heads of nigella, rudbeckia, echinacea, poppies and scabious are plentiful. Now is the time to cluster seasonal blooms with seed heads, herbs and seasonal fruits and vegetables to make unique arrangements in the Dutch flower-painting style. During the last months of the gardening year the colour palette becomes more limited among seasonal blooms, so you may need to consider more commercial cut flowers mixed with seasonal textures and leaves. Grasses mixed with the last of the summer roses, dahlias, hips and berries make for an arresting display.

If you don't want to be bright or showy, choose a late-season meadow feel with cow parsley, *Daucus carota* 'Dara', flowering mint, hydrangeas, eryngium and grasses. Spike it up in muted colours with garden roses or Metallina, Blue Gene, Hypnose, Amnésia and Quick Sand roses. Hydrangeas in all their colours are at their best and most available in this season. I adore the lace-cap varieties and the delicate green 'Annabelle', and now is the best time for *Hydrangea paniculata*. These conical-shaped hydrangeas have a fresh virginal quality, in stark contrast to the brash yellows, reds and purples of the late summer flower harvest. 'Kyushu' is cream and 'Limelight' is very green.

Left Collars of seasonal dahlias adorn church columns, with hydrangeas, old-fashioned chrysanthemum blooms, trails of ivies, cotoneaster berries, clematis vines and rosehips.

CARTHAMUS TINCTORIUS 'KINKO'

NASTURTIUM

LEONTOPODIUM ALPINUM (EDELWEIS)

NIGELLA DAMASCENA SEED HEAD

ECHINACEA

PRUNUS SPINOSA (BLACKTHORN)

ALLS)

ASCLEPIAS CURASSAVICA 'SILKY GOLD'

ROSA 'RED PARTY'

DAHLIA 'HOWARD RED'

DAHLIA 'TANBURO'

RUBUS FRUTICOSUS

ECHINACEA PURPUREA 'WHITE SWAN'

DAHLIA 'INDIAN SUMMER'

HYDRANGEA ARBORESCENS

NASTURTIUM

ACHILLEA 'PAPRIKA'

SOLIDAGO 'GOLDREDEL'

SYMPHORICARPOS 'CHARMING FANTASY'

CRASPEDIA GLOBOSA (BILLY BALLS)

HELIANTHUS MINI

DAHLIA

VIBURNUM TINUS BERRIES

ASTRANTIA MAJOR 'CLARET'

HYPERICUM

MATTHIOLA INCANA CENTRUM 'CARMINE'

ARTICHOKE

ROSA PUMPKIN HIPS

KNIPHOFIA 'ALCAZAR'

AMARANTHUS CAUDATUS 'CYCLOPS'

SETARIA ITALICA 'RED JEWEL'

Autumn

The ripeness of autumn brings with it a bounteous cornucopia of textural fruits, vegetables, nuts, seed heads and some very showy flowers. This season still offers some striking seasonal blues and mauves, such as aster daisies, aconitum, artichoke flowers, hydrangea and ornamental purple cabbages. These look great with dark red gladioli and hanging amaranthus. Of course, the palette can be very cheery and fiery, with eremurus, kniphofia, chrysalis, achillea and sunflowers. I am drawn to yellow in the spring and again at this time of year, when I can use crocosmia berries and flowers with sunflowers, particularly the double 'Teddy Bear' varieties and the burgundy and chocolate varieties. It is also a great time for pinks, with nerines, *Amaryllis belladonna*, bouvardia, astilbe, astrantia, dahlias, sedum and pink snowberries. Autumn offers the chance to do bold mixes with textural foliages, berries and grasses. Gerbera daisies in autumnal tones work well with pincushion proteas and roses.

It is not a time of year when I naturally think of white, as the gardening season ends and we are all thinking of more earthy and organic tones. However, I have designed some stunning white weddings in September and October. My personal preference for a white wedding scheme in autumn would be against a backdrop of autumnal foliages and textural seed heads. It would include showy white dahlias, tall gladioli, Oriental lilies, delicate lysimachia, frothy dill, white snowberries, white ornamental kales and white *Euphorbia fulgens*. As the trees turn red and lose their leaves, we are enticed by the warm shades of red and orange and fall in love again with dramatic and bold designs. There is nothing I love more at this time of year than to use glycerined beech leaves with seeded eucalyptus, long rosehips, crab apples, solanum and aubergines. Old-fashioned bloom chrysanthemums such as 'Tom Pearce' and blowsy dahlias add a vintage autumnal look.

Right A mossed candelabra groans under the weight of the autumn's harvest, with small apples and artichokes. Purple campanula and burgundy dahlias contrast with orange marigolds and physalis lanterns.

ROSA 'FAIR JEWEL' HIPS

CAPSICUM ANNUUM

CURCURBITA GOURD

AUTUMN

ARBUTUS UNEDO

ROSA CANINA HIPS

...ASSIC' HIPS

CARTHAMUS TINCTORIUS 'KINKO'

CALENDULA OFFICINALIS 'KABLOUNA'

VIBURNUM OPULUS 'COMPACTUM' BERRIES

MALUS

BRASSICA OLERACEA 'CRANE PINK'

ACHILLEA FILIPENDULINA

NIGELLA

ACONITUM 'SPARK'S VARIETY'

TRACHELIUM CAERULEUM 'LAKE TAHOE'

PHYSALIS ALKEKENGI 'JUMBO'

Below A wonderfully textural and colourful bouquet with mixed dahlias, astrantia, cotinus, craspedia, *Alchemilla mollis*, rudbeckia, eryngium and flowing *Miscanthus sinensis* 'Malepartus' grasses.

Winter

Winter weddings can be very cosy, atmospheric and magical. Winter wonderlands are a common theme, and also at this time of year many want to take advantage of the short day by having candlelight everywhere. Candlelight is so flattering and terribly romantic. Red and burgundy feature a lot, as do cream, brown and apricot. It is a great time of year to feature a metallic colour in your decorations and there are many foliages, seed heads and twigs that are dipped in gold, bronze and silver on the market. For a white winter theme, I often use amaryllis, cut phalaenopsis orchids, ranunculus and roses. Rosemary and eucalyptus make great scented foliages for this time of year.

Seasonal flowers to look out for are *Euphorbia fulgens*, which has arched stems with tiny florets and come in whites, creams, oranges, reds and burgundy. Cymbidium orchids are in season and make good corsages and wedding bouquets as well as wonderful showy feature flowers in pedestals. I am very often drawn to the fruits and vegetables around at this time. I love the small waxed and glittered fruits that go through the huge Dutch auctions. I also enjoy decorating candelabras with sparkling birch twig, or enhancing displays of amaryllis with gold contorted willow. Gilded Savoy cabbage has been an enduring delight in this season, too, often filled with 'Naomi' red roses.

Of course, for a more rustic and low-key wedding scheme, foliage is an obvious way to go. Ivy, mistletoe and spruce can be used with natural cones and cinnamon to great effect. This also provides a wonderful scent for your event. I also love berries and hips, and holly berries in red and golden yellow are a seasonal highlight. Skimmia, both in flowering and berried form, also adds some colour. I often use variegated foliages in winter, though not in other seasons.

Spring flowers also start to come back onto the scene and so it is a great time of year for commercially grown narcissus, hyacinths, anemones, ranunculus and tulips. For the scented winter wedding, pots of jasmine and gardenia are available, as well as fragrant freesias.

Opposite A posy of *Leucojum vernum* snowflakes makes a delicate bouquet.

HELLEBORUS 'CHRISTMAS GLORY'

HIPPEASTRUM 'CHRISTMAS GIFT'

FORSYTHIA X INTERMEDIA 'SPECTABI[LIS]'

LARCH

NARCISSUS

VIBURNUM TINUS

BLUE PINE

HELLEBORUS

CYCLAMEN

GALANTHUS

PRIMULA

CYMBIDIUM 'YONINA'

Above A headdress with ivy leaves, ivy berries, sprigs of *Viburnum tinus* black berries and flowers in bud, *Rosa* Red-Eye (sometimes also known as Ivanhoe) spray roses and rosebuds from *Rosa* Red Sensation.

HEDERA

SALIX CAPREA 'SNOW FLAKE'

MOSSED LARCH

GLOSSYPIUM (COTTON)

ILEX VERTICILLATA 'OOSTERWIJK'

ROSA 'FAIR JEWEL' HIPS

SKIMMIA JAPONICA 'RUBELLA'

ROSMARINUS OFFICINALS

EUCALYPTUS PULVERULENTA 'BABY BLUE'

BRASSICA OLERACEA 'WHITE CRANE'

LIGUSTRUM BERRIES

Index

Figures in italics refer to captions.

Acknowledgements

This wonderful book has taken two years to put together and has been a labour of love. I have worked with a very special team on this book; they are my friends as well as talented work colleagues. None of this would be possible without my publisher, Jacqui Small, whom I have had the pleasure of working with for twenty years. Most grateful thanks to Jacqui Small and all in her office for their support and hard work. Enormous appreciation to my patient, loyal and long-serving editor, Sian Parkhouse, for going above and beyond just editing on this project! I was delighted to work on this book with Tim Winter who gave this project his all. Tim and his assistant Dave Foster both made the long shoot days fun and produced some beautiful images, as well as adding their creative and artistic input. I am indebted to Robin Rout, the creative genius on this book, for designing it so beautifully. I am also very grateful to Charles Miers from Rizzoli, who has published all my books in the United States, for his loyalty and support.

A huge debt is owed to all the below for their help in making this beautiful book:

Photography
All photography is by Tim Winter apart from the following:
Page 6 Catherine Simmons and Ian Cohen: photography by Julie Kim
www.juliekimphotography.com
Lucetta Johnson and Alex Moylan: photography by Alexandra Papakonstantinou
Sam and Jono Farmer: photography by Peter Jenkyn peter@jenkyn.co.uk
Page 8 Liz and Enda McCarthy: photography by Jamie Bott www.jamiebottweddingphotography.com
Beverley and Chad Carlson: photography by Chris Grover www.fotonovo.com
Shanyan and Matthew Koder: photography by www.filmatography.com
Page 9 Penny Lancaster and Rod Stewart: photography by Sim Canetty-Clarke
www.simphotography.com
Shanyan and Matthew Koder: photography by www.filmatography.com
Page 169 Jamie Bott www.jamiebottweddingphotography.com

Cakes
CakesbyKrishanthi for the beautiful cake on pages 228–229 www.cakesbykrishanthi.co.uk
Anne Cadle for the elegant cake on pages 230–231
Mich Turner of Little Venice Cake Company for the gorgeous cake on pages 118–119
www.lvcc.co.uk
Rosalind Miller for the fabulous cake on pages152–153 www.rosalindmillercakes.com

Venues
Guy and Liselle Chisenhale-Marsh for being so generous to my team and me and being so enthusiastic about weddings
Gaynes Park, a wonderful wedding venue, perfect in every way. www.gaynespark.co.uk
Laura Caudery for allowing us to shoot at the elegant and unique Fetcham Park
www.fethchampark.com
www.parrallelvenues.co.uk

Thank you to Nicola Pottage and Kelly Zuber and all at the Concerto Group
Oxo 2, London www.oxo2.co.uk
Charles Howard and all at The Jockey Club Newmarket www.jockeyclubrooms.co.uk
www.sudeleycastle.co.uk
www.blenheimpalace.com
www.thersa.org
www.villadurazzo.it
Abbey Gardens, Bury St Edmunds

Growers and Flower Suppliers
Thank you especially to Richard Ramsey for the dahlias and help with the captioning.
www.withypitts-dahlias.co.uk
Loek and his Dutch growers and Peter De Mos Kees from Select Flowers www.selectflowers.nl
All our suppliers at New Covent Garden Market and thanks especially to:
Dennis and all at www.dennisedwardsflowers.com, all at Porters Foliage, GB Foliage, S Robert Allen, Pratley Covent Garden, Quality Plants Ltd
Our Italian growers and in particular Sacha Cepollina sacha.cepollina www.ciesseflower.com

Venue Stylists and Production
I am also very indebted to Ilknur and Levant Tekinbas from Mediterranean Occasions. They are both the most creative, resourceful and patient people I have had the pleasure of working with. Thank you to Mediterranean Occasions for the Mandap and styling on page 200, draping on page 211, chair covers on page 204, chuppah on page 199. I am also very grateful to talented Mehmet Ozdemir for the bespoke chair covers on page 43
www.mediterraneanoccasions.co.uk

Invitations and menu cards
Cutture www.cutture.com

Churches
St Mary Le Bow in Cheapside, London
wwwstmarylebow.co.uk
Our Lady and St Alphege, Bath
www.saintalphege.org.uk
St Mary's Church, Cheveley, Suffolk
www.cheveleygroup.org
St Mary's, Dalham, Suffolk
St Mary Magdalene, Woodstock, Oxfordshire

Props
The Libra Company www.thelibracompany.co.uk
www.serax.com
www.despots.nl
www.dkhome.com
www.lsa-international.com
www.cbest.co.uk
Great Hire www.greathire.co.uk
Well Dressed Tables
www.welldressedtables.co.uk

Weddings
From *Summer in the City*, I would like to thank: Sonya Pollitt for introducing me to Kathy and Phil and for input on the wedding scheme. Wedding party: Menna Hawkins, MadeleineThompson, Caris Newson, Neil Graham, Jon Duncanson, Edward Matten, James Dowler, Alexander Milne 1 Lombard Street and their event organizer Filli Fält www.1lombardstreet.com
Roz and Dave Cleevely for their gorgeous

Glowing Garden in Cambridge:
www.byardart.co.uk
www.gelupo.com
Sarah Hammond and all at Rhubarb
www.rhubarb.net
Wise Production for their vision and production.
www.wiseproductions.co.uk
Julia Dowling of Snapdragon
www.snapdragonparties.com
www.husandhem.co.uk
for our Scandinavian inspired wedding.
Bitte Stenström for Spira Haga fabric
Tom and Clare Gray for the beautiful wedding in Bath and all their guests who were very good sports! Laura & Stuart Heath (bridesmaid and husband); mother of the groom Sue Gray; James Gray and Daniel Gray, sister and bridesmaid Catharine Collingridge; mother of the bride Eugenia Collingridge; father of the bride Peter Collingridge; sister-in-law and bridesmaid Helen Collingridge; niece and flower girl Grace Collingridge. Ushers: William Houghton, Christopher Harlow, Michael Brown, Craig Bourke, Jon Lockhart, John Collingridge, James Gray, Kit Patrick, Oli De Groot. Confetti throwing: Suzanna Lyons and Michael Brown, Lorna Logan, Meera Chadha, William Hooke, Muiris Moynihan, Stuart Lee Archer, Anthony and Philip Reed, Esther Okusaga and Tobi Weiloch
Lady Annabel Goldsmith
Always a pleasure to work with London's finest caterers, James Hurworth, Robert Salter and Glynn Woodin from www.mustardscatering.com
Sally Lancaster
www.designbyappointment.com
From *Hot Pink Shades* thanks to Gaynes Park – the ceremony was held in the Orangery and the reception in the Mill Barn. The arch on page 205 is in the Gather Barn. www.gaynespark.co.uk

Brides and grooms
Philip and Kathryn Wright
Clare and Tom Gray
www.claretherese.com
Sam and Jono Farmer
Shanyan and Matthew Koder
Liz and Enda McCarthy
Lydia and Mike Halliday
Lucetta Johnson and Alex Moylan
Rod Stewart and Penny Lancaster
Catherine Simmons and Ian Cohen
Beverley and Chad Carlson

Models
Aaron Briggs, Katie Cochrane, Jemma Jerez, Scarlett Lander, Chloe McKernam, Nell Pizey, Hayley Pryke, Kate Pryke, Anne Romaniuk, Elizabeth Romaniuk, Eliza Stokes, Sally Stokes, Phoebe Winter.
Not forgetting our four-legged friends: Connie, Cosmos, Lily and Frankie

Paula Pryke Flowers
www.paulapryke.com
Thank you to my loyal, talented and supportive staff. Great teamwork and enthusiasm as always. Wendy Boileau, Anne Cadle, Katie Cochrane, Jo Cook, Anita Everard, Gina Jay, Eunah Kim, Sawa Kindo, Tania Newman, Penny Pizey, Jamie Price, Hisako Watanabe, Karen Weller, Tae-Yoon.
Our most humble thanks to all my wonderful clients, the ultimate source of our passion, creativity and livelihood.